lifeGIVING MENTORS

a Guide for Investing Your Life in others

Tim Elmore

Forward by John C. Maxwell

www.GrowingLeaders.com

Published by Growing Leaders, Inc.
270 Scientific Drive, Suite 10
Norcross, Ga 30092
www.GrowingLeaders.com
ISBN 981-04-9914-0

contents

This chapter provides definition to mentoring and how it may appear in everyday life. It reveals the two popular approaches to mentoring, what should be the goals of a healthy mentoring connection and how to build a foundation for a mentoring relationship.

This chapter communicates the necessity of life on life investment, and how intimacy, accountability and real impact can only be achieved in mentoring communities. It differentiates between small (fellowship) groups and mentoring communities and how mentoring accomplishes unique goals

Everyone needs a mentor—but for different reasons. The young need it because they lack experience. The experienced need it because it is so easy to fall into ruts. This chapter will focus on why it's so strategic to focus on investing in the emerging generation.

If we're going to focus on this next generation, the Millennial generation, we need to know who they are, how they think and what they need. This chapter will provide a quick profile on a new generation of students and what they most need from a mentor.

Men often approach mentoring differently than women. This chapter highlights their strengths, then communicates the typical challenges in mentoring for the male gender. It closes with a list of practical steps men can take to become more effective communicators.

Women frequently possess qualities that enable them to mentor effectively. They also face specific challenges to overcome based on their gender. This chapter identifies their strengths and weaknesses, and provides practical tips to improve female mentoring skills.

Everyone needs a mentor, including mentors. This chapter relays the criteria for selecting a mentor or coach that fits your identity. It gives practical insights as well as a checklist you can use in your own selection process.

This chapter shares the criteria for selecting a mentee or protégé that fits your style of leadership and strengths; one that can benefit most form the value you bring to a relationship. It gives practical insights as well as a checklist.

contents

contents

forward

I have been interested in leadership my entire adult life. During my forty plus years as a corporate executive, founder of a not-for-profit organization, and pastor, I taught leadership not only to my staff, but to hundreds of thousands of other executives, coaches, presidents and pastors across the country.

One of the conclusions I've drawn is that the art of mentoring is all about practicing the functions of a leader, in a single relationship. This handbook on mentoring will be a literal guide to you, as you seek to lead people, one life at a time. Tim Elmore and I have had hours of conversation and application on this issue, and we both believe that mentoring is the first and last task of a leader. It is the first task of a leader because everyone who wants to lead the "masses" ought to begin by leading one person. It is the last or ultimate task of a leader because the acid test of any leader is—are they able to reproduce themselves in others? Success without a successor is a failure. Both leadership and mentoring are about multiplication. Both are about developing people.

I love Tim Elmore. He and I have been in a mentoring relationship ourselves, for more than twenty-five years. He is now communicating the principles that he practiced as a leader in San Diego, Denver and Atlanta—to hundreds of thousands of other leaders around the world. I can promise you that you will be enriched with every chapter you read from this comprehensive manual. It is literally an encyclopedia on mentoring. It will act as a sort of "mentor" to you on how to mentor others. May you go on to add value to others as you develop them, and multiply yourself in them.

Dr. John Maxwell
Founder, The Injoy Group / EQUIP

how to get the most out of this book

Some would say that mentoring is just a fad, just a buzzword that happens to be popular in our generation and within our culture.

I disagree. I am obviously elated about the current interest in mentors connecting with protégés. But I believe it is much more than a trend. The fact of the matter is every lasting movement in history has been sustained through two vehicles: (1) the values and distinctives of that movement were committed to paper, and (2) the initial leaders mentored a second generation of leaders. John Wesley, for example, employed both of these vehicles as the great Methodist movement took root over two hundred years ago in England. He was committed to mentoring young preachers and setting up "class meetings" (accountability groups) to nurture spiritual growth in his followers. I still remember visiting Epworth and Bristol in England and seeing the results of Wesley's mentoring system. He built a chapel in Bristol where he could watch (from a glass window above the sanctuary) his young, emerging ministers as they preached. Later, he would meet with them and evaluate their progress. It is my belief that this is what gave permanence to his movement. George Whitefield, a contemporary of Wesley, never experienced this kind of legacy. George Whitefield was a more sought after public orator and drew the largest crowds of any preacher in his generation. John Wesley, however, was committed to reproducing leaders; he determined to mentor young men. In one of his last statements, George Whitefield said that Wesley had outperformed him. Why? Wesley had trained young leaders everywhere in England and America. Sadly, Whitefield confessed that his followers were "a rope of sand."

The purpose of this handbook is simple. I am not attempting to replace the magnificent books that have already been written on the subject of mentoring. As you turn the page in a moment, you will see I have cited some of the best books on mentoring from our own generation. I have tried to do the homework for you and glean from the best practices taking place around the U.S. and the world. These books are a "must read" as far as I'm concerned.

What I am attempting to do is provide a practical and speedy reference book, to be glanced at over and over again, as you engage in the practice of mentoring. There is not a large amount of philosophy to wade through here. Instead, there are handy insights and easy-to-use lists to implement that have been tested and proven over time. I have laid out the material in a "question and answer" format, drawing from the most qualified experts in the field as well as my own experience and observation. This is literally a bottom-line reference book on the subject. In fact, I will suggest four different ways this book could be useful to you:

1. Read it through for your own personal enrichment.

2. Use it as a source to train others in the art of mentoring.

3. Study and discuss it in a small group setting.

4. Utilize it as a reference guide as you encounter questions.

My goal is to provide practical "handles" to theoretical truth. I want to mentor you in the art of mentoring.

Here is my conviction for doing so. I believe we cannot accomplish our ultimate work and leave a legacy without investing in next-generation leaders. And we cannot mentor en masse. It cannot be done with thousands in an arena. We have all seen the big "programs" in business, non-profits or local churches where we've attempted to "disciple" people in "assembly line" fashion, cranking out committed team members from a conference or classroom setting. I don't believe that's the most effective method for producing leaders. If it were, we would have plenty of healthy leaders today.

While I do believe there is a place for the classroom or for conferences, real workers and leaders are best developed through life-on-life mentoring. It requires making deposits in people, one life at a time. It is about forming a learning community involving experiences and relationship with each other. It's what Confucius did with his followers. It's what Socrates did with his students. It's what Jesus did with his twelve disciples.

That is what this handbook calls you to be and do. It is difficult. It is slow. It often seems like poor stewardship of your time. But with the right individuals, the payoffs are extraordinary. I am speaking of a "movement" not a program. Programs usually start big...and then, as their novelty wanes, they fizzle and become small. Soon, we have to begin looking for a new program. Movements, on the other hand, generally start very small...and become huge! Let's begin the adventure now.

"PLEASE MENTOR ME"
an open letter from the next generation

It is an image indelibly etched into the American consciousness: four of the fastest men in the world poised at the start of the 4 x 100 relay at the 1988 Olympics. Comprised of a peerless group of athletes, each a champion in his own right, it was inconceivable that the United States team could lose. Yet as the final leg of the race approached, the unthinkable happened. The Americans dropped the baton. Quick as lightening it was over. The race and any hopes of a gold medal were lost. The crowd, electrified moments earlier, was struck mute. All the potential nullified because of a botched hand-oft.

For many of us who fall in the age group known as the "Millennials" or "Generation Y" (born between 1984 and 2002), this disastrous scene aptly describes the sense of loss we often feel entering adulthood. We are different than the last two generations. Searching desperately for mentors to teach us, yet not knowing where to look, we are left feeling like runners stranded at the starting gate without a baton. Some may characterize us as lazy "slackers," or "self-absorbed idealists," but the truth is...ours is a digital generation—we stare at a screen much of our day. We lack direction and identity; we're often missing a sense of continuity with our heritage. We are fuzzy because so many options lie in front of us. Some of us have been the "trophies" of our parents but they never let us grow up. Most of us move home after college. It underscores our need for mature men and women to come alongside us, to share their wisdom, and hand us the torch of leadership for our generation.

In the ancient scriptures, we find that a young man, to be considered a true Jew, was required to trace his lineage to Abraham. They knew their family heritage. Yet many of us growing up today scarcely knew our own fathers. We appear over-confident—but it's often a front. We're going every direction. We lack guidance and focus. We're confident about our dreams but don't have much experience. We need you. When we appear distrustful, it is because we have been disappointed so often. We hunger for your friendship. We thirst after someone with strong character.

We ask ourselves: "Where are the men to accept us with no strings attached, to let us serve alongside them—without fear of failure? Where are the men willing to share their mistakes so that we might not repeat them? Where are the men willing to love us enough not to leave us the way we are?"

ix

Will you take a risk with us, and allow us to serve alongside you in the fight for values we all face? Will you let us share with you our burning passions, while receiving the treasure of your experience? Bridging the gap is not as hard as you might think...all we're really asking for is some coaching to help us get past our childhood and enter the adult world. Our generation will lead this culture into the next century. We need you to help us find our place in a confusing world. Please don't leave us standing at the starting gate.

Signed,

Looking for Mentors

x

I have to admit, I was a little proud. My good friend Rob had just won the award for being "Teacher of the Year" at the high school where he taught. I had the privilege of attending the banquet that would honor him.

At the close of the evening, he was asked to make a speech disclosing what his "secret" was for impacting students. Everyone seemed to wonder what made him unique. Just how had he made such a difference in their lives? Rob stood poised at the small oak podium, prepared to answer these profound questions. He cleared his throat and began to speak. He told stories of students who had made right choices about their lives and literally engineered a turnaround for the good. As he concluded, he attempted to summarize his part in the process: "I guess my secret was that I made the move from merely being a teacher to being a mentor to these teens."

Indeed, he had. I had personally watched him all year making priceless investments into the lives of those young people. And tonight, Rob was saying a mouthful. He had become a mentor to so many of them. There was a strange quietness in the room that night. Although no one said it out loud, I am certain the majority of the audience didn't get it. I think they were filled with unspoken confusion: What's the big secret? What's the difference between a teacher and a mentor? The truth is there is often a marked difference in our Western society. While every mentor is, indeed, a teacher, not every teacher is a mentor. I heard a statement years ago that was so profound I decided to make it a personal core value. It goes like this: More time with less people equals greater impact for everyone.

It sounds wrong. If it is right, it certainly is counter intuitive. Think about it for a moment. If I choose to mentor — not just teach — I'm choosing to limit the volume of people I can meet with at one time. But, I can better multiply myself in them. The transaction goes from informational in nature to transformational. The person I mentor is impacted more profoundly, and he's more likely able to reproduce the experience in someone else.

coming to terms

No doubt, the term "mentoring" has become a popular "buzzword." Unfortunately, it has accumulated various definitions on its road to fame. At Rob's award banquet, there were dozens of images that raced across the minds of his audience when he used the word. We all seem to be on different pages.

It will serve us well, then, to offer a working definition at the beginning of this handbook. I have tweaked a definition first developed by Paul Stanley and Robert Clinton:

> **Mentoring is a relational experience through which one person empowers another by sharing their wisdom and resources.**

The resources vary. Mentoring is a positive dynamic that enables people to develop potential. Since the rash of leadership failures between 1995 and 2005, more people recognize the need for accountability in leadership. Adequate mentoring might have prevented most of these failures. Certainly the kind of mentoring described in this handbook can help prevent failures in leadership and give that needed accountability. Leaders want to finish well. They would welcome mentoring if they saw it as an enhancement to their growth. Mentoring can reduce the probability of leadership failure, provide needed accountability and empower a responsive, potential leader. John C. Crosby of The Uncommon Individual Foundation writes, "Mentoring is a brain to pick, a shoulder to cry on and a kick in the seat of the pants."

In their book *Connecting*, Stanley and Clinton continue with this helpful perspective. Usually when people are first introduced to mentoring, they think of an ideal mentor — a perfect model who can do almost everything. Few of those exist. The myth about mentoring is that it requires some hyper-gifted guru, just dripping with wisdom. A sage. A Moses or Socrates figure. Those people are few and far between. In this handbook we want to put mentoring in the practical realm: Anyone can mentor, provided he/she has learned something from the past and is willing to share with others what he/she has learned.

I remember my first attempts at mentoring. I was filled with the usual sense of inadequacy as I considered what to say to someone that could actually change their life. I finally had to scrap my original stereotypes of white haired, all-wise mentors and simply begin a relationship with someone that I felt I was a step or two ahead of in my own journey. I ended up choosing seven high school students. We met together each week for a structured meeting and then enjoyed several informal experiences that bonded us relationally. All seven of those students became leaders. Three of those seven became executives. The other four became missionaries or ministers. Soon I was mentoring interns where I worked. What a joy it is today to see them leading companies, managing nonprofit organizations, counseling, teaching, working as missionaries and serving in the government or in charitable organizations. I feel like a proud parent!

As an adult, you can mentor others. Whatever you possess — wisdom or a personal strength — that has enabled you to deepen your influence, you can pass on to others. For example, introducing a young professional to the basics of career success is a type of mentoring. There are career mentors, academic mentors, spiritual mentors, financial mentors and personal coaches or mentors. You need to know that there are various styles of mentoring too. According to my research, there are more than a half a dozen different kinds of mentors that can play a role in someone's life. We must stop stereotyping. In Chapter 12, I outline these different kinds of mentors, noting that we all need a variety of them based on the stage of life we are experiencing. In addition, we will naturally flourish serving as a certain kind of mentor (to someone else) based on our own personal identity.

Reading about the heroes of the past, or historical models, is another form of mentoring that can happen anytime. Observing the growth, struggles, responses and decision-making processes of those who have lived before can provide insight, challenge and often practical help for our own situations.

Consider this. Occasionally, a person may enter your life who makes a timely contribution: some wise counsel, an insight, a question or a word of encouragement. This can be considered a mentoring moment. Mentors come for a reason, a season or a lifetime. These "divine contacts" will not usually know how they are being used in your life, but you can take advantage of them as resources that arrive at the right moment. They are, in fact, a sort of mentor to you. This will probably be true for you as well, as you assume the role of a mentor.

3

There will be moments you will share a simple insight or truth (that you may have picked up years ago), and doing so, you will change the perspective of your mentee forever! There will be times you will "speak into their life" with authority and wisdom — and not realize how profound your words really are. Simply put: People mentoring people is the greatest method for transforming the world!

mentoring through the years

Interestingly, mentoring is not a new concept. For example, mentoring happened in some form in ancient Greek and Hebrew cultures. Both had their own "model" for making disciples. The term "mentor" actually originates from ancient Greek mythology. The Greeks made it an art. There were disciples everywhere. For instance, the philosopher Plato was a disciple of Socrates; and Aristotle was a disciple of Plato; and believe it or not, Alexander the Great was a disciple of Aristotle. What a great line of minds and postulates and hypotheses. Their disciple making process, however, was different than that of the Hebrews in the scriptures. The method and focus was distinct. It is the Hebrew model I am advocating here in this book. Let me explain.

While Americans have embraced the Greek model for learning, the Hebrew model is the cry of this new generation. The Greek model is what I call the "classroom" model. It is about words and information. Even when the Socratic method is used, it's still about a teacher delivering content.
This takes place each week when teachers assume their place up front, and students passively listen to a lecture. It is academic in nature; it is cerebral and cognitive.

It is often passive on the part of the student. And while it is the fastest method to transfer information to another person or group, it is not the most effective method for transforming a life. It is not the preferred mode for today's students to learn. Learning happens much more efficiently through the Hebrew model, where the teacher or mentor invites the student to travel with them. No doubt, the mentor has much to say through verbal instruction, but this is not the only tool in their pocket. They demonstrate the principles they want their mentees to embrace in a real life context. Then they let those mentees try their hand at it themselves. They understand that the best way to learn is to experience something firsthand. Finally, they give time for debriefing and feedback. They provide accountability and assessment. In short, the following table summarizes the contrast between these two learning models:

GREEK MODEL	HEBREW MODEL
The Classroom Model	*The Coach Model*
1. Academic	1. Relational
2. Passive	2. Experiential
3. Theoretical	3. On the job Training

Obviously, these two learning methods received their titles from the culture in which they were originated. Long before Jesus came along and chose twelve men to mentor, the ancient Greek culture was making disciples, as I've mentioned, with Socrates and Plato, Plato and Aristotle, etc. But the mentoring was much more philosophical in nature than with the Hebrew culture. It was more academic than relational. While there was the Socratic method of dialogue involved, it was more passive than experiential. It was, in fact, much more like the classrooms of our schools and churches across the United States than what Hebrews did in ancient Israel. For instance, it would have been common to ask a student from the Greek culture the question: "What subject are you studying?" This would also be very common in our American colleges today. In the Hebrew culture, however, the question was not, "What are you studying?" but rather, "Who are you studying under?" The emphasis was on the mentor not the material. Most of us are familiar with the Hebrew model and perhaps don't even know it. Consider the most popular historical mentoring relationship we know of today.

Jesus and his twelve followers. Jesus treated his disciples or mentees more like apprentices than academicians. They received "on-the-job training." You can imagine how that must have accelerated their learning curve! Can you visualize how much more quickly Simon Peter must have grasped how Jesus dealt with difficult situations when he knew he might be asked to do it the following Thursday? The fact of the matter is: This is what good "mentoring" is all about. It is recognizing that humans "own" principles much more quickly when they are learned from relationship and experience than from a sterile classroom.

the evolution of education

Mentoring is as old as civilization itself. Through this natural relational process, values and experience pass from one generation to another. Throughout history, mentoring was the primary means of passing on knowledge and skills in every field — from Greek philosophers to English blacksmiths — and in every culture. Mentoring took place among Hebrew priests (Eli and Samuel), prophets (Elijah and Elisha) and leaders (Moses and Joshua). But in our day and age, the learning process has shifted. It now relies primarily on computers, classrooms, books and videos.

Thus, the relational connection between the knowledge-and-experience giver and the receiver has weakened or is nonexistent. Society is now rediscovering that the process of learning and maturing needs time and many kinds of relationships. The "self-made" man or woman is a myth and, though some claim it, few aspire to it anymore. It leaves people relationally deficient and narrow-minded. The resurgence of mentoring in virtually every occupational field and area of life is a response to this discovery. "Please mentor me," is the spoken and unspoken request expressed by so many today.

CASE STUDY: HELEN KELLER

Most Americans are familiar with the story of Helen Keller. Helen was the blind, deaf and dumb mute who acted more like an animal than a human in her early years. She would have grown up to be nothing more than a vegetable if left alone. She was so unruly that her family hired a teacher named Anne Sullivan to mentor her. Their goal was to simply enable Helen become healthy so that she wouldn't damage the people or things in the house. Anne entered her life early on and began to work with Helen on her vocabulary, personal habits, perception/recognition, manners and speech. Anne's inspiration was Helen's own growth from a disabled mute to a valuable citizen in society. Because she had been transformed, she determined she was going to help others...like Helen Keller. By the time Helen reached adulthood, she was a changed woman. When the two of them met, young Helen was in a cage and would only growl at her new mentor. By the conclusion of Anne's work, Helen was communicating efficiently, eating by herself and taking care of her own personal needs. Anne Sullivan had brought about an absolute revolution in Helen Keller, and helped to build a self-sufficient woman.

This wasn't the end of the story, however. In the later years of her life, Anne Sullivan had a relapse of her previous condition. She became physically ill and went blind. Ironically, now the "mentor" was in need of someone to work with her again. Can you guess who stepped forward to fill the role? It was Helen Keller. She returned the favor to her mentor; she was able to give back to the one who had given so much to her.

Like all good mentors, Anne Sullivan illustrates a number of the specific ways that mentors help mentees:

- *Ability to readily see potential in a person*
- *Tolerance with mistakes and abrasiveness in order to see that*
- *Potential develop*
- *Flexibility in responding to people and circumstances*
- *Patience, knowing that time and experience are needed for development*

- *Perspective — the vision to see ahead to suggest the next steps a mentee needs*
- *Gifts and abilities that build up and encourage others; they*
- *Empower mentees*
- *Timely words of counsel and insight, even when it requires correction*
- *Resources such as letters, articles, books, contacts with others, etc.*
- *Opportunities for that young mentee to gain experience on their own*
- *Evaluation — taking the time to assess the progress of the mentee*

the bottom line

Most mentoring stories share some common features. They started with someone in need. This person met someone further along in experience who had something to contribute to that need. A relationship was established. The more experienced person shared what he had been through or learned, meeting the needs of the first person. With the acceptance of what was shared, the power to grow through a situation was passed from the mentor to the mentee. It was not just a sharing and receiving of information — actual change took place. We refer to this transfer between mentor and mentee as "empowerment." This process is the heart of mentoring.

Mentoring is popular at present. Its popularity attests to its potential usefulness for leadership development. It also speaks of the tremendous relational vacuum in an individualistic society and its accompanying lack of accountability. In Habits of the Heart, the authors see individualism as an American asset turned into a liability. Americans cling to personal independence when they desperately need interdependence. I don't believe people are at their best when they are self-sufficient, moving through life alone. To experience healthy "community" will require recognition of this need and the courage to change. In no other area is this change so urgently needed than in leadership development. Acknowledgment of this need is partially responsible for the groundswell of interest toward mentoring. The question: "Will you mentor me?' is being expressed in a variety of ways in every arena: business, family, military, education, politics and the church. This swelling cry for meaningful relationships can be a springboard to learning and growth via the art of mentoring.

life giving mentors: the road less traveled

I no longer think the need is merely for mentors. I believe the need of the hour is for "life giving" mentors. We need life-giving leaders, bosses, teachers, pastors and coaches. To understand this idea, it's best to examine the two most common roads that educators travel.

7

You can tell almost instantly if a mentor is on the traditional path or the "road less traveled." In the Jewish Pentateuch, we read about the Garden of Eden, which contained the Tree of Life and the Tree of the Knowledge of good and evil in the center of it. These two trees represent two different approaches to life and teaching: one is life-giving; the other, life-grabbing. The two most common paths are...

LIFE GRABBING
1. Stress and competition
2. Thrives on rule and routines
3. Narrow and rigid
4. Teaches subjects
5. Asks: What do I have?
6. Success built on competence
7. Focus is on techniques
8. Imposes control over mentees
9. Goal is to complete the lesson plan
10. Acts out to duty and obligation
11. Content oriented
12. Repulsive: I keep score
13. Result: Tired performance

LIFE GIVING
1. Innocence and peace
2. Thrives on relationship
3. Open and relational
4. Teaches students
5. Asks: What do they need?
6. Success built on connection
7. Focus is on atmosphere
8. Expresses confidence in mentees
9. Goal is to complete the student
10. Acts out of devotion and gratitude
11. Change oriented
12. Magnetic: I keep giving
13. Result: Empowered service

observations on these two approaches

Let me take a moment and offer some observations on this idea. Life giving people make the best mentors. However, time usually takes its toll on us. As we age, we tend to get cynical. We no longer keep giving — we keep score. Examine these statements and see if you agree with them.

1. We often begin our career as life-giving, but drift into a life-grabbing posture over time.

2. As we progress in leadership, we take pride in our competence more than our connection.

3. Leadership built upon rules is easier to implement than leadership based upon relationship.

4. Academic pressure or economic pressure fosters life-grabbing habits and attitudes.

5. It is possible to discipline students and even fire staff while in a life-giving posture.

6. *Life-grabbing people seek to be in control; Life-giving people seek to be under control.*

symptoms of life grabbing leadership

A school or organization that is managed by a life-grabbing perspective may appear on the surface to be fit as a fiddle. However, upon deeper examination, you find these symptoms:

1. *Leadership nitpicks and keeps score on others, both staff and students.*

2. *Leadership is empty of power and offers no joy to staff or students.*

3. *Leadership is suspicious of the worst in students and lays plans accordingly.*

4. *Leadership's goal is merely damage control rather than trusting students with authority.*

5. *Leadership doesn't believe in faculty and students nor does it bring out the best in them*

6. *Leadership is more like a police force than a training ground.*

7. *Leadership is unable to develop and multiply quality leaders.*

the heart of life giving vs. life grabbing mentors

I will be honest with you. I have a "Tarzan gift." I can jump from tree to tree, back and forth, several times a day. In the words of the Pentateuch again, I move from the "tree of life" to the "tree of the knowledge of good and evil." One moment I can be life-giving, and the next I can be rigid and grabbing all the life I can get from others. I may start the day believing the best about others, but by noon, I am suspicious and calculating again. This makes me very unattractive to others, including my mentees. I have attempted to summarize below the "heart" of both approaches.

LIFE GRABBING MENTORS	LIFE GIVING MENTORS
1. Life is scarce	1. Life is abundant
2. You play Defense (Maintain)	2. You play offense (Create)
3. Escape loss	3. Pursue vision
4. Reactive	4. Proactive
5. Guard and protect	5. Risk and seize opportunity
6. Paralyzed: Hold on!	6. Dynamic: Let go!
7. Does the bare minimum	7. Walks the "second mile"
8. Thinks: win / lose	8. Thinks: win / win

9

My hope is that as you pursue emerging leaders to mentor, you will approach your role from a life-giving perspective. Life giving people are irresistible.

Our organization, Growing Leaders, Inc., for instance, has seen the results of positive mentoring.

A student in Cairo, Egypt who was mentored decided to return the favor by beginning an orphanage in his homeland.

Two students, in their senior year of college, launched a leadership training event on their campus in 2002 that still exists today, challenging fellow students to become life-giving leaders. This event now attracts dozens of other schools.

A student in Indonesia became angry at the sex trade among children in Southeast Asia. At the encouragement of his mentor, he decided to launch an organization that would locate these kids, rescue them and rehabilitate them.

A student was so transformed by understanding his life-mission that he has created a networking website reaching hundreds of thousands of other young adults to help them identify their calling and connect with others like them.

A high school student who watched a television program on slave trade in the Sudan and Uganda decided he could not allow that injustice to continue without getting involved. He found a mentor and gained the confidence to launch a movement that raises money to set slaves free in those African nations.

I hope you sense something of the potential that mentoring may have for you in unleashing the insight in your life through special relationships with others. Perhaps you are beginning to sense that you want to establish relationships with others that will make a difference. May this be said of you as you mentor others.

a mentor is a people grower

He has a sort of green thumb when it comes to handling folks.
He'll listen to their troubles; He'll chuckle at their jokes.
Somehow they know his interest is genuine and true,
And right before your eyes you'll see them grow an inch or two.
You'll see their faces blossom out in smiles of budding cheer.
You know they've found a ray of hope you drive away their fear.

You know he's sowed the seeds of faith and showered them with love,
And made them sense the presence of the good Lord up above. He
clears out all the weeds of doubt and fear and hate and greed
He gives them room to breathe. He seems to sense their every need.
He nurtures them with praises for the good things that they've done and
trains them to look upward
And to stand tall in the sun.
He has a sort of green thumb like a farmer with the sod
But his work is growing people in the image of his God.
~Author unknown

Probably the greatest word picture for what mentoring is all about can be summarized in the little story of a boy and his dad walking down a rocky road one evening. After stumbling and falling to the ground, the boy looked up at his father and said, "Dad, why don't you watch where I'm going?" I believe we can say with great accuracy that this is what mentoring is all about - watching where others are going.

before you go any further...

Before you tread any further through this handbook, let me ask you some questions. Please reflect on them prior to reading the next chapter. Consider these questions as friendly accountability. I want to ensure, as much as I can, that this book won't simply provide mental stimulation, but mentor application!

1. Do you have any transparent relationships (friendships)? Who are those people?

2. Do you have people fulfilling these roles for you?

    a. A Mentor? _____

    b. An Accountability Partner? _____

    c. A Mentee? _____

3. Do you know one or two people that could benefit from your mentoring?

4. What would be the best way to approach them? What might be the best time?

Is mentoring really necessary? Wouldn't it be possible to pull off our jobs and prepare future leaders without all the trouble it requires? Is it possible to impact the people around us and not bother with "one-to-one" mentoring?

These are good questions. They are ones that leaders have knowingly or unknowingly been asking for hundreds of years. Reflect with me for a minute on history.

Consider colonial times in England and Europe. In past centuries, master tradesmen deliberately chose young apprentices to work alongside of them. It wasn't because those young men increased their profits immediately or sped up their work. My guess is it took longer to get a job done when the master blacksmith attempted to teach someone the trade. But the master was intentional about placing an apprentice nearby because he knew his trade was always one generation away from extinction. He knew one day he would need help. If he didn't develop someone else, his practice would cease when he died. These kinds of apprenticeships helped businesses move forward. There was no formal program or classes — just mentoring.

Consider the Dark Ages. Society was shaped by both political leaders as well as church leaders. During this period, all but a small portion of the Church world refused to make such personal and painstaking investments. Interestingly, the practice of mentoring began its decline with Constantine's reign.

In 313 A.D., when Emperor Constantine declared Christianity the official religion of the Roman Empire, Church members began to choose the easy route. The practice of faith moved from organic to programmatic. It became institutionalized. Parishes began to rely on the paid clergy to do ministry. The making of disciples, through mentoring relationships, came grinding to a slow crawl. Eventually, Christianity came to be associated with stained glass, impersonal worship services and institutions. I believe this contributed to society's plunge into the "Dark Ages." Any mentoring that did occur was predominantly confined to monasteries and disassociated from society at large. There were few life-giving relationships. Unfortunately, this left the Church in a pitiful state of ignorance and compromise, which affected society as a whole.

How about today? Is mentoring making a difference on our culture? Consider this: I read recently that one half of the Nobel Peace Prize winners last year were mentored by former Peace Prize laureates. Is that a coincidence? I don't think so. The Harvard Business Review ran a cover article in 1983 entitled "Everyone Who Makes It Has a Mentor." The article reported a study of the top Fortune 500 executives in America. Each of them was asked questions to determine what they had in common. It was a wide variety of executives — male and female, old and young, single and married, self-made and family-groomed. Interestingly, only one answer came up every time. Can you guess it? Every one of these CEO's said they had a mentor. Each had someone they could call in the middle of the night, if need be, to seek their wisdom and counsel on tough issues.

This is why Growing Leaders, Inc. has included MENTORING as one of our core values. We follow that value with this descriptive phrase:

> **MENTORING**
> **Leaders cannot be mass produced but**
> **are developed through life on life mentoring**

the great need on campus
I believe mentoring is no longer a mere luxury among a few students today. Mentoring is an essential element for students to not only survive but to also thrive in the world they're entering. They need the wisdom and encouragement that experienced adults can give.

14

The great need on the school campus today is: developmental relationships. These are relationships that exist for the purpose of growing the individuals over an extended period of time. Students cry out for a "coach" more than a classroom. Why? Let me suggest another phrase I am convinced of after thirty years of mentoring:

There is no life-change without life-exchange

We all need mentors — but for different reasons based on the life-stage we are experiencing. I need certain kinds of mentors early in my career and different kinds later in life. Reflect on these two statements below:

1 We need mentors when we're young because we lack experience.

2. We need mentors when we're older because we fall into ruts.

The different life stages require different kinds of mentors, for different reasons, but we all need mentors all of our lives.

do you want to impress or Impact people?

Do we really need the art of mentoring? It depends on your goal. Consider this truth: Leadership can be viewed on three levels. From least effective to most effective, these levels may be defined this way:

Level One: *Impress*
The leader impresses followers. This can be done with little or no relationship. It requires only the will of the leader to be involved. He must want to leave a memorable impression on the followers. It can be done at a distance — a concert, a conference, a convention.

Level Two: *Influence*
The leader influences followers. This can be done with some relationship between the two. It requires the will of the follower to be involved. He must want to be influenced by the leader. This usually involves a connection between leader and follower at some point.

Level Three: *Impact*
The leader impacts followers. This can only be done through intimate relationship. It requires both the will of the leader and follower to be involved. They must agree to accountability and growth. It usually happens up close and personal.

15

Notice that all three levels change the follower in some way, but life-change dramatically increases as the conditions of level three are met. Level one can be done within the context of the masses, level two requires a bit more relationship and commitment, but level three can only occur when both parties agree to connect and commit to each other. Impact requires some form of mentoring.

At this point in my life, I have intentionally mentored over three hundred people, either one-on-one or in a small group. I have failed as often as I have succeeded in being and doing exactly what my mentee needed at the moment. I have cringed and cried when I've thought about some of my earlier days attempting to "pour my life" into someone but not knowing just how to do it. Thank God for merciful mentees who were happy to gain whatever they could from someone like me. As I reflect for a moment, however, I am convinced of at least one truth: No matter how poorly I played my role as mentor, those relationships were always better than if I'd only performed on some platform in an auditorium. In other words, even my feeble attempts at mentoring are better than my best attempts at impressing someone from the stage. Good, honest attempts at developmental relationships are better than no attempts at all.

Students today don't want a "sage on a stage" but rather a "guide on the side."

Author Dawson Trotman popularized an axiom decades ago that has directed the course of many successful training programs. He followed it during his career and mentored many great leaders before his death over fifty years ago. Great leaders throughout history demonstrated this principle time and time again with their followers. It could be called the Principle of the Narrow Wedge. Read it over a couple of times. It goes like this:

"More time with less people equals greater impact for everyone."

what makes mentoring unique?
Mentoring is unique from most educational programs in that it is so focused. The surest way to secure your impact on people is to enter an accountability relationship with the conscious objective to produce measurable growth. This cannot be done with large groups. In fact, most small groups in residence halls, corporations or churches today don't mentor people well. Fellowship, love and nurture are all naturally fostered in them, but true mentoring is conspicuously absent.

So often we define mentoring in broad, all-inclusive terms and miss what is really meant by the practice of developmental relationships and life-on-life investment.

For instance, while it is possible to inadvertently mentor someone in the course of normal academic programming, it is rare. Mentoring usually does not happen effectively in a large lecture hall, a typical Sunday school class or even an average small group community. Consequently, as you consider mentoring people in a small group context or group leadership training, please note the distinctive characteristics of a mentoring relationship below. The following is a table that contrasts what normally happens in a small group versus what happens in an effective mentoring relationship. While there is some overlap in the relational focus, note the differences that set mentoring apart from fellowship groups. My challenge to you is to become a true mentor to the people you serve.

Small Groups	Mentoring
1. Focus on relationships	1. Focus is on giving and receiving direction
2. Context is community	2. Context is personal
3. Discussion oriented	3. Application oriented
4. Normal size: ten to fifteen	4. Normal size: one-on-one to one-to-three
5. Value depends on the attendees	5. Value depends on the group mentor
6. Content based on the leader	6. Content based on the need of the mentee
7. Leader's goal is collective	7. Mentor's goal is intentional growth investment
8. Progress is often sporadic	8. Progress is made by predetermined goals
9. Success measured by group health	9. Success measured by life change of mentees
10. Low level of accountability	10. High, intense level of accountability
11. Community (heart and mind)	11. Direction and leadership (heart, will and mind)
12. Purpose is to meet and interact	12. Purpose is to reach potential

Very often, two people enter a mentoring relationship — where one determines to help the other reach their potential — but alas, the relationship eventually reduces itself to fellowship. Mentoring is more emotionally expensive than fellowship. We naturally migrate to "small group" relationships but must intentionally work at mentoring relationships. Sometimes, it is hard work.

Consequently, the answer to the question, "Is mentoring really necessary?" can only be answered when we respond to a second question: How deeply do we want to impact people? I trust your answer to both questions will lead you into deep reflection.

becoming relevant for an epic generation

Let me give you one more reason why I believe mentoring is so essential today. Students are growing up in a very different world than the one I grew up in. Their attention spans are low, their demand for hands-on experience is greater, and their expectations for their education are high.

One way to avoid a mentee's loss of interest or lack of commitment is to maintain a high level of relevance as you interact. Not only should mentors keep the conversation on the key issues facing their mentee, but you should also transmit truths in an EPIC fashion.

Becoming an EPIC Mentor

E – *EXPERIENTIAL* (They don't want a one-way lecture, but an experience)

How can you practice this style of teaching and mentoring?

P – *PARTICIPATORY* (They want to participate in the outcomes of the meeting)

How can you practice this style of teaching and mentoring?

I – *IMAGE DRIVEN* (They grew up with MTV, Digital cameras, DVDs and video)

How can you practice this style of teaching and mentoring?

C – *CONNECTED* (They are connected technologically and relationally)

How can you practice this style of teaching and mentoring?

The traditional education style of lecture, drill and test is declining fast. As Dr. Leonard Sweet reminds us, students today have moved form a Gutenberg world to a Google world. This gives me all the more incentive to become a relevant mentor.

At Growing Leaders, we sponsor an event on college campuses called: The Habitudes   Experience (Habitudes   are images that form leadership habits and attitudes). The event is a portable conference that challenges students to think and act like leaders.

In this event, we attempt to foster mentoring relationships between adults and students. The day is an EPIC day, as we reveal leadership principles using a variety of mediums:

- An image on the screen
- Music
- Video
- Dramatic sketches
- Activities
- Interviews
- Small group discussion
- Panels
- Journal Time

While it is a lot of work to host these events, they are much more memorable than the typical "talking head" conference, where one speaker monopolizes the time up front. May you do the work necessary to connect with your students today.

19

I recognize it sounds cliché, but we are living in exciting times.

I began working with students back in the 1970s. Those students made up the tail end of the Baby Boomer generation. This generation was known as the anti-establishment generation. They questioned authority. Through the 1980 and 1990s, I worked with the Baby Busters, or Generation X. This generation was known as the disillusioned and disconnected generation. They ignored authority. Today, we are working with Generation Y, or the Millennial generation — students born between 1984 and 2002. They are an optimistic, digital and an overachieving generation. They choose their authority.

In short, Millennials are much more likely to work with established authorities than the previous generations — but they will choose them based on their credibility. They are actually looking for mentors and are determined to find them so they can reach their lofty goals. They think out of the box and need mentors to give them a moral compass and a sense of reality. I can summarize the last three generations with these statements:

Baby Boomers asked: Why?

Generation X asked: Why ask why?

Millennials ask: Why not?

a summary of the millennial generation

Let me share the good news and bad news about this generation — and why it is so crucial to focus on them as mentors. Let's begin with the "good news." The following list is the result of research we've done with eight organizations in an attempt to summarize the qualities of Generation Y, or specifically the Millennial generation:

the good news

So how many of them are out there? The Millennial generation promises to be the largest generation in American history. Already, they rival the Baby Boomers in size (78 million), and with immigration, there may be upwards of one hundred million of them before they all reach adulthood. Worldwide, they are massive. About half the world's population is twenty-one years old or younger. The following is a list of characteristics:

they feel special

Movies, government focus and parents have all made this generation believe they are vital to our future. Most of them feel good about themselves. In fact, they're often preoccupied with themselves; however, some surveys found a contradictory self-assessment — they are happy with their lives, but they worry a lot about themselves and their future. Their self-absorbed lives can be alarming. On Mother's Day 2006, USA Today carried an article on what young people were giving their moms for her special day. Thousands had decided to give themselves something in honor of their mother. The gifts ranged from getting a haircut, to putting money in their own bank account, to cleaning up their apartment. And the mothers were pleased with those gifts. Their children played such a central role in their own happiness, that mother's felt great about the vicarious gift.

they love family

They rely on family as a sanctuary from the troubles of their world. They've been sheltered by many kid-safety rules and devices. They grew up with the "Baby On Board" sign on the mini-van. Many are the focus of what I call "parental paranoia." The result? They love their family. If they aren't a part of a nuclear family, they create one (i.e. gangs and unorthodox communities). In a recent annual U.S. survey of teenagers, students were asked: Who is your hero? For the first time in twenty years, the number one response was not an athlete. Number one was: mom and dad. Number two was: grandma and grandpa.

they are confident

Millennials believe they can make a difference. Many already boast about their power and potential, even as kids. They will be more self-reliant and ambitious than Generation X. A surprising percentage has started their own business before reaching age twenty-one. They don't seem to lack the confidence to put their ideas into action. Many believe they will take part in changing the world. In one recent study, 82% of college students said they believed the next "Bill Gates" was in their generation. 51% said they believed they knew the next "Bill Gates." 24% said they believed they are the next "Bill Gates."

they are mediavores

These students are addicted to media. It's not uncommon for them to do homework, listen to a CD, watch TV and interact online simultaneously. They give new meaning to multi-tasking. They can handle fast-paced images in commercials, and they love the rush of high speed internet searches, text messaging their buddy or locating friends on Facebook. No doubt, there is a danger to their familiarity with technology. One private university I recently visited reported that 60% of their male students were watching pornography on the internet. And an equal amount of women were participating in chat rooms, which can be just as harmful. Technology is a mixed blessing, but they are addicted to it.

they are team oriented

Think about it. They grew up with Barney, played soccer, learned in groups at school and often wore uniforms. Community is as important as individual accomplishments. Many date in groups. Some only want a leadership position if they can serve alongside a team and share the responsibility. On the DISC profile, one research study discovered that almost half of these Millennials indicated they were high "I" in the test. They are people-persons. They love relationships even though their people skills are often poor. One book called Bowling Alone suggested a difference between Baby Boomers and Millennials. The book said while Baby Boomers are bowling alone on Wednesday nights, Millennials are playing soccer in teams.

they are global

This generation promises to build relationships all over the world. They will be the most mobile group ever. They have itchy feet and want to travel, just like they have on the internet.

Those involved in a local church can attest to the fact that short-term mission trips are on the rise and have been for over fifteen years. Young people want to experience a new culture and what life looks like around the world. 50% of the Millennial generation surveyed plan on doing some of their college studies overseas. They want to travel and experience new places and people each year.

they are pressured
They've been pushed to study hard, avoid personal risks, and capitalize on opportunities their family has afforded them. Schedules are tight for them and their parents; they live with stress. I saw a cartoon recently which showed two school girls leaving the field after soccer practice. One of them said to the other: "Wow! You got fifteen minutes between soccer practice and violin lessons? What are you gonna' do with all that free time?" Whether its pressure from parents, school testing programs, coaches or themselves— these students feel the stress of being a super-kid. They've been pushed to make the grade, make the team and later, make the money. The outcome of this is ill-adjusted adults. Just five years ago, a book was released entitled: Quarter Life Crisis. The book reports a parallel to the "mid-life crisis" from the Baby Boomers. There's an alarming amount of twenty-five year olds who are clinically depressed and seeing a therapist because they reach their dream as quickly as they'd hoped.

they are harmonious
For the first time in decades, this generation is cooperative and conventional. They take pride in improving their behavior and often are more comfortable with traditional values than parents. George Barna believes there are at least twenty different teenage subcultures existing in the United States today. Teenagers often belong to multiple subcultures. Sometimes because they are transitioning from one to another.
Sometimes because they have multiple interests that require variety in their tribal loyalties, and sometimes because they are searching for their place in the larger culture. However, while we still hear about high school shootings from time to time, this generation has experienced far less of that sort of thing than in the previous generation. For instance, at Columbine High School, the two killers might have had a huge trench-coat mafia group to identify with had they attended school twenty years earlier. At Columbine in 1999, however, the school was full of cheerleaders and jocks. They just didn't fit in and the only recourse they felt was logical was violence.

they are generous

They not only enjoy accomplishment, but they also enjoy giving away their resources. They want to serve their communities. 50% of teenagers are active in community service; they feel it's their duty. I have been in missionary festivals where an offering is received for a missionary couple who was about to leave for their international assignment. I have marveled when those offerings have been upwards of $50,000. Students will empty out their purses and wallets if they see a cause worth giving to. One government study reported that the average teenager has $87 a week to spend. For many, it's easy come, easy go. Sadly, these same students possess a financial knowledge deficit. More than half admit they have no financial knowledge; only 5% feel very knowledgeable. Both high school and collegians affirm that their parents are the #1 influence on finances. Half of college students owe at least $10,000 in student loans. The average graduate owes more than $20,000.

they are optimistic achievers

They may be the best-educated, best-behaved adults in the nation's history. They are full of hope. They aren't as cynical as Generation X. They want to make a difference; optimism drives them. While the last five years has seen a drop in this optimism (since 9/11/01) from the former fifteen years, there is still a sense in which Millennials are saying: "Yes, the world is messed up — but we are going to fix it." Unlike the previous two generations, they believe the world can and will get better. Sometimes, this flies in the face of wisdom. It has been said: Generation X struggled with authority. Millennials struggle with reality. This just might be true. But their unwavering optimism has already driven them to action. In 1997, an Aurora Elementary School divided all their fifth and sixth grade students into small groups. Then, they gave each of these small groups a different geographical region of the world to study and write a paper. One group of 10-11 year old kids received Sudan, Africa. They had no idea what kind of horrific place the Sudan is to live. Torture, civil war, religious persecution and slave trade are still going on in that nation. When those students discovered that slave trade was still going on today, they pushed their paper aside and began to talk. One student boldly asked: "What are we going to do about this?" Then, without any prompting from adults, they brainstormed how they could address the problem. Finally they came up with a solution that worked for them. They began to pool their allowance money and put it in a kitty. Then, they found an organization online that received donations and with them bought slaves and set them free.

That little group of students began sending their money in, and one by one, they set slaves free in Sudan. By year's end, they had held fundraisers and raised $50,000 for the cause.

As I reflected on this, I thought to myself how unique these kids are. If that had happened when Baby Boomers were kids, we would have demonstrated or rioted or held a sit-in. Generation X would have written some angst-filled song about the whole thing. But the Millennials are doing something positive to change it.

the bad news

Unfortunately, the news is not all good news. While this generation promises great potential for good, when we examine what's happening globally, it is sobering. Every year, I am in front of between 50,000 and 60,000 students, staff and parents talking about this next generation — who they are and what adults can do to mentor them well. It always makes for a lively question and answer time.

One question seems to come up everywhere: What is happening around the world? In other words, are there any international trends we can spot that let us know what is coming in this generation of kids? I must confess, I certainly don't have the final answer to this question, but let me share two sobering facts that ignite me to work even harder to provide a moral compass for students today:

FACT: Today, almost half of the world's population is twenty-one years old or younger.

While people are living longer, the birthrate is passing older generations — in some countries at an alarming rate. Today, the average age in China and India is mid-twenties. Many people in African nations won't even see their 30th birthday because of the AIDS pandemic. As I mentioned, in the U.S., the Millennial generation is already rivaling the Baby boomer population in size, at seventy-eight million. Some sociologists say it may grow to one hundred million strong in the U.S. due to immigration. We are a reflection of the globe. The earth's population is growing younger, and they desperately need guidance.

FACT: When there is a bulge in the youth population, there is always violence.

Gunnar Heinson, a social scientist at the University of Bremen (Germany), writes that when 15-29 year olds make up more than 30% of the population, violence occurs; when large percentages are under fifteen, violence is often imminent.

The causes for such violence can be immaterial. Whether the country is rich or poor, whether they experience good conditions or bad, violence and passion follow a bulging population of young people. This explains Ireland ninety years ago. It explains Africa over the last fifty years. It explains Latin America in the 1980s and Europe in the 1500s. For that matter, it explains the violence America experienced in the 1960s. It was primarily the young Baby boom population rioting on the university campuses or in the streets.

what will come of this youth bulge?

Today, there are sixty-seven countries where a "youth bulge" exists (that is, populations where more than 30% are young adults or kids). Sixty of those countries are presently in civil war or are experiencing mass killings. Heinson has written an eye-opening book called, Sons and World Power. In it, he documents this history of youth and violence. It matters not if the countries are civilized or non-civilized. It is more about the next generation finding a place to express their identity. Without healthy guidance, they'll join any cause and enter into anarchy. Don't believe me? Just watch them. Of the twenty-seven biggest "youth bulge" nations, thirteen are Muslim. Those kids will find expression even if they take it out on the rest of the world.

The U.S. has been involved in Iraq for years now. It provides a sobering case study. Like many of its neighbors, nearly half of the population in Iraq is under eighteen years old. According to Iraq's Ministry of Education, 70% of elementary school kids are no longer attending classes regularly. Hassan Ali, a sociologist at the Ministry of Labor and Social Affairs says, "These children will come to believe in the principles of force and violence. There's no question that society as a whole is going to feel the effects in the future..." This generation of kids in that part of the world is growing up unemployed, undereducated, traumatized and, among boys in particular, ripe for vengeful appeals of militias and insurgent groups. According to Newsweek magazine (January 22, 2007), it isn't only the Iraqi kids either. From the Middle East to Europe to America, violence may well beget violence around the world for years to come. French scholar, Gilles Kepel, author of Jihad: The Trail of Political Islam, warns that many of these young people, raised on anger and fear, are potentially rebels without clear causes. "What will their jihads become?" he asks. "Are they going to grow up to kill each other, or will they turn their weapons against the West?"

27

Very often we blame the poor conditions of such countries in conflict. Not so. In El Salvador, for example, the explosion of political killing in the 1970s and 80s was preceded by a 27% rise in per capita income. Poverty wasn't the problem. In reality, the problem is that in a youth-bulge society, there are not enough positions to provide all these young men with prestige and standing. They want to be known for something. In America during the 1960s, college campuses were scenes of demonstrations and riots that often ended in violence. The issue wasn't poverty — the U.S. was experiencing a healthy economy. So what was it about? No doubt there were a variety of reasons, but one that's often overlooked is the Baby Boomers were coming of age. We had a youth bulge. Young people long to find expression. They want to make a difference...and they will... whatever that means.

Globally speaking, it appears this next generation will provide a clash between optimism and nihilism. Students from high technology nations, full of optimism, plan to give their lives to improve the world's conditions. Yet, there are young people — especially from terrorist countries — giving their lives up in order to take the lives of others. They are the ultimate in nihilism.

Here's my point: If we're serious about transforming the world, we have to be serious about investing in this next generation. Here's my question: What are you willing to sacrifice to invest in them? What we do today as adults will no doubt determine who they will become as adults.

I've lost count of the adults I've seen who have thrown their arms up in the air, in despair over this new generation of kids and said, "Ah! Kids today! They're worse than ever!"

While this statement may be coming from an adult who's simply speaking from their personal experience, statistics are clear that this statement is wrong. If you examine what's going on nationwide, you'll see that this new generation of young adults are, indeed, different – but in a good way. Their grades, their behavior and their passion to change the world has gone up. Teen pregnancy, drug use and alcohol abuse have gone down. These kids may prove to be much more valuable to society than either of the last two generations. They may be the best educated, most informed generation in history. In fact, for the first time, this generation doesn't need leaders to get information. Thanks to the internet, an audience of kids can know more about a subject than the speaker does. What they need is leaders who can help them interpret the information they receive. In other words, they don't need leaders to access data. They need leaders to process data. That's where mentors come in. We hold the key. If we're going to focus on this next generation, the Millennials, we need to know who they are, how they think and what they need. Let's take a look at how their brain works and how we can connect with them.

how do they like to communicate?
Several months ago, we hosted another focus group of students (ages 16-24) and asked them: What are your preferred methods of communication?

We thought it was a good question. After all, we're all about trying to connect with this Millennial generation, so we thought we'd ask just how they wanted to receive our messages. Their response shouldn't have surprised us.

Their top eight methods of communication are:
- Text messaging
- Internet (i.e. MySpace.com or Facebook.com)
- iPods and Podcasts
- Instant messaging
- Cell phone
- DVD / CD
- Books
- Email

I want you to notice a few things about this list. First, note that email is last on the list. One student described email as "a way to communicate with older people." Second, with one exception, this list moves from more personal to less personal in nature. They want something customized, not generic, if they're gong to pay attention. Third, and most importantly, these students prefer a "screen" for six out of their top eight favorite methods of communication.

the screen age

While all generations share common characteristics, each generation is defined by some shared elements in their developmental years. The primary elements that define a generation are:
- Shared music
- Shared experiences
- Shared crises
- Shared television programs
- Shared celebrities (people of influence)
- Shared age and era

Today, the delivery of almost every one these elements share one thing in common — they are driven by a screen. Call me the master of the obvious, but students want to interact with a screen. In fact, we've begun to call students "screenagers" because they are more at home in front of a screen than watching a talking head on a stage. They want a personal message but want to control how intimately vulnerable they become. They like the option of control.

The fact that text messaging landed at number one on the list tells us a lot about students today. Bear with me as I venture some observations about why text messages are the preferred method of communication:

1. Text messages represent very current communication.
   More so than voicemails, a text means I need to interact now about something relevant to you.

2. Text messages are generally sent from someone you know.
   Unlike phones, you generally don't get a "wrong number" or generic call on a text message.

3. Text messages are brief and to the point.
   The person texting doesn't waste words; in fact, they usually abbreviate the message.

4. Text messaging is in your control. The receiver can stop when they want to.
   This kind of control is attractive to students today. They want communication on their terms.

Students today are inundated with messages from every side. I believe they're most likely to respond to a text message because it allows them fast, current, relevant communication with friends — but at a safe distance. They like intimacy without a lot of vulnerability. It sounds like a paradox, and perhaps it is. I believe this is but one of several paradoxes that exist among Generation Y. That's why I reminded you already: This is the first generation who does not need authorities to access information. Why? They have screens. However, they do need authorities, like you and I, to help them process that information. This is our challenge.

a comparison and contrast of two generations
Millennials represent a shift from the mindset of the previous generation, the Baby Busters (or Generation X). While some characteristics remain the same, I believe major changes have taken place as the Busters have given way to the Millennials. Let me compare and contrast the two generations below.

Comparison Between Generation X and Generation Y
Both love community
Both appreciate authenticity
Both recognize the world is messed up

Both hunger for better, more healthy families
Both are at home in the world of digital technology
Both learn best through images, relationships and experiences

Contrast Between Generation X and Generation Y

Generation X (1965-1983)	Generation Y (1984-2002)
1. Anti-establishment	1. Work within establishment
2. Angered by their broken world	2. Challenged by their broken world
3. Cynical and jaded	3. Optimistic
4. Struggles with authority	4. Struggles with reality
5. Wants to escape their problems	5. Wants to fix their problems
6. Movie: *Reality Bites*	6. Movie: *Pay It Forward*
7. Ignores leadership and authority	7. Chooses leadership and authority
8. My job is irritant	8. My career is a place to serve
9. Who cares about transcripts/ resume?	9. Load up the transcript and resume
10. I'm not interested in leadership	10. I plan to change my world

millennials: the pros and cons of generation y

For ten years now, sociologists have been surveying students from the Millennial Generation. Authors Howe and Strauss drew some early conclusions about them in the year 2000. Some of them remain the same; others have changed as we move further into the twenty-first century. In other words, the later Millennials are a bit different than the early Millennials. Let's take a look at the pros and the cons of this generation today. Each of the positive qualities has a negative consequence and vice-versa. Sometimes, these pros and cons collide or contradict each other. For instance, in 2000, 90% of Millennials planned on going to college. By 2006, however, 30% of them didn't even finish high school. What we must do, as mentors to this generation, is help them capitalize on the "pros" and diminish the consequences of the "cons."

PROS	CONS
1. They feel special and needed	1. They can act spoiled and conceited
2. They own the world of technology	2. They expect quick and easy results
3. They love community	3. They often won't act outside of a clique
4. They are the focus of their parents	4. They may be unable to cope with reality
5. They are high on tolerance	5. They often lack absolute values
6. They've had a fairly easy life	6. They lack stamina to finish high school
7. They catch on to new ideas quickly	7. They struggle with long-term commitment
8. They can multi-task	8. They often can't focus on one central goal

9. They have a bias for action and interaction
10. They want to be the best
11. They plan to live a life of purpose
12. They are confident and assertive
13. They hunger to change the world

9. They're too impatient to sit and listen long
10. They can get depressed when they aren't
11. They often neglect tasks that seem trivial
12. They can come across careless and rude
13. They anticipate doing it quickly & easily

a summary of the recent shifts in millennial minds (from 2000 to today)

- They have become more cautious and a bit more anxious about the state of the U.S.
- They want to be change agents, but see the pace of change will be slower than desired.
- They're unhappy and even pessimistic about the present direction of politics/economy.
- They are questioning their former obsession with good grades and college acceptance.
- They have begun to see they have little understanding of stewardship of time or money.
- They want to explore the future but can be paralyzed when faced with so many options.
- They hate society's moral decay but most now admit to cheating at school/on resumes.
- They're often at odds with their own beliefs/values and feel they must grow up too fast.
- They're dissatisfied with US leadership (corporate & government) unlike 5 years ago.
- They feel ill-prepared for life after school, and often return home after college.

principles to apply when communicating

Let's step into the minds of this next generation. Based on our interaction with about 50,000 students a year and our research with Generation Y, let me share some of our conclusions about how to communicate with them as a teacher or mentor.

33

If You Want Your Message To Stick, Remember...

1. *Students learn on a "need to know" basis.*
   Don't just jump into your topic; take time to explain the relevance of it. Why should they listen?

2. *The less predictable your words, the more memorable they will be.*
   Once you summarize your point, ask yourself: Is it cliché? Find a fresh way to say it, with a new twist.

3. *The first 4 minutes must grab their head or their heart if you want sustain their interest.*
   Be quick to get to some content or reveal your own heart. Provide a reason for them to listen.

4. *The more "in your face" your words are, the more trust you will earn.*
   They love to "speak their mind" and tend to trust communicators who are blunt like this.

5. *If you challenge the status quo, they will hunger to take a journey with you.*
   They have high expectations of themselves and of anyone "up front." Challenge the norm.

6. *They grew up loving images, so give them a metaphor.*
   Their world is VH1, video games, photos, DVDs and the internet — you must have a picture, too.

7. *Once you prepare your message, you must find a way to twist it to exceed their expectations.*
   Think about movies or novels that stick; they excel by adding another layer of story.

8. *For your message to remain retained, keep the pace of change high, and call them to change.*
   Change is key. Their world is changing fast. They love change; your talk must be full of changes.

9. *Teach less for more.*
   This sounds contradictory, but it isn't. To be remembered, plunge into one central theme.

10. *Remember, students today are both high-performance*
and high maintenance.
Walk the delicate balance between nurture & challenge.
Help them "own" your message by building a bridge of
relationship that can bear the weight of truth.

our takeaway: what do we do?

So, what do we do? If these reactions are true, how can we help
the Millennial generation respond well to the needs of the world
around them? Let me suggest a few:

1. Let them be different from Generation X. They want to create
a new reality. Things lose their novelty fast for students today.
Don't chide them — encourage them to be themselves and
define their own identity.

2. Help them to make and keep short-term commitments.
Millennials have a tough time making long-term
commitments since everything in their world has been so
instant. Help them get a win under their belt, which will lead
to a longer, deeper commitment.

3. Challenge them to take their place in history. We need them
to make a contribution to their community and to the world
at large. Give them a sense of destiny. Talk to them about
heroes from history (historical mentors), especially ones that
come from the elder generation.

4. Work with them to simplify their lives. Often, Millennials will
induce pressure on themselves to be perfect, all at once, in
every area. They have a passion to make a difference and
get all they can out of life. They must learn to simplify and
figure out what really matters...and enjoy the process.

5. Communicate that there is meaning even in the small,
mundane tasks. Give them a sense of the big picture and
how all the little things they do fit into the story of God and
His redemption of the earth. Provide a macro view in their
present micro world.

6. Enable them to set realistic goals. You will find they often
possess lofty dreams, and they need help turning them into
bite-size objectives with deadlines. Don't rain on their parade
— just help them take realistic steps, one at a time toward
their target.

7. Help them to focus. Millennials often become fuzzy because they scatter themselves so thin, in a variety of different activties. They don't want to miss anything life has to offer. Work with them to focus on one meaningful objective and pull it off.

8. Work with them to develop personal values. I believe this should come before vision. They live in an eclectic and pluralistic world. If they are not value-driven, they will shift as they encounter pressure from the culture.

9. Resource them with your network. Their dreams will require your assets. We can accelerate their growth with the networks older generations have established. If nothing else, this meets a special need for them to nurture good people skills. They love community but they often lack relational maturity.

10. They long for mentors who are genuine and accessible. Based on assessments we've done at Growing Leaders, mentoring communities are the preferred way they want to learn. As I've mentioned already, they don't want a sage on the stage, but a guide on the side. They want a hero they can talk to.

our summary of generation y

This generation is sometimes called The Mosaics. They don't think in a linear manner but like a computer would store information. It is a mosaic menu of icons in their minds. They can live with contradictions; they are overloaded with information, and they are exposed to graphic information earlier than previous generations. The vast majority thinks about their future weekly and is trying to figure out their purpose in life. Parents are the greatest influence, over peers, teachers or youth pastors. Many have been pampered and their optimism may make you sick. In a 2000 survey, it was discovered their number one goal is education, and they believe one person can make a difference in the world. Almost half are the "Influencing" style on the DISC test. They want to invest their life in people and change the world. Their most glaring flaw is a realistic perspective on what it will take to do this. They struggle with reality. The adult generation must fill the role of mentor, and coach them, channel their passion and strengths until they have accomplished what they are able to do. Well Known Millennials: Dakota Fanning, Haley Joel Osment, Britney Spears, Michelle Kwan, Kerry Underwood, Lebron James, McCauley Caulkin, etc.

Their Fears and Concerns:

1. *They list the need to grow up faster among the biggest disadvantages of being part of their generation.*
   Many finish college and return home to live with their parents for the next three to four years. They are waiting to grow up and find the perfect job and mate. They want to pursue a calling not just a career.

2. *They're not happy with the direction of the country.*
   Sixty-two percent of Millennials believe the general direction of our country is heading the wrong direction. They are more conservative politically than their parents (most of the time), but they don't like the divisive, angry politics going on today.

3. *In some ways they are at odds with their own beliefs and values.*
   They're struggling with their spirituality; faith is important to them, but organized religion is a turn-off. When asked who they would like to have dinner with (living or dead), Jesus Christ remains the number one sought after dinner guest, with almost twice us many votes as others in prior studies.

4. *They don't see the world in black or white; right or wrong.*
   Most think littering is absolutely wrong, however only half of those same students say it's absolutely wrong to exaggerate on a resume or not declare all of one's income on an IRS form. They often possess situational ethics. They want to possess values, but life has been very convenient for them, with a need for little sacrifice.

5. *They want their life to count.*
   Nine out of ten of them think about the future several times a week. They desire a "life of purpose" and want to engage in work that has a higher meaning than to merely draw a paycheck. They're trying to make sense of it all, but life gives them an anxious eagerness about the future.

the time is now

As we examine the make-up of this next generation, it appears the time is ripe to develop them as leaders. They are predisposed to want to make a difference and long to live a life of purpose. It seems they are primed to leverage their influence in the world, if we will just mentor them.

Over the last six years, "Growing Leaders" has surveyed thousands of students, all Millennials. Based on our findings, as well as those of the Kellogg Foundation and Coca Cola, we offer the following conclusions regarding students and leadership development:

- Leaders are made, not born.
- Students require a catalyst to begin the leader development journey.
- Becoming a leader is a process not an event.
- Students learn leadership best in communities.
- Students need a guide to help them process their experience.
- In today's world, every student will need leadership skills.

It dawned on me sometime during the summer of 1989. My wife and I had celebrated eight years of marriage together, but it had just struck me how differently she and I approach life and relationships. I had become serious about providing healthy leadership in our home. I try to assume responsibility for the health and development of my relationships. With this in mind, I had begun to negotiate with my wife, Pam, just how I could enhance her personal development. How could I help her grow?

After setting some goals together, I determined we'd reach those goals as strategically and swiftly as I knew how. I wanted to get her from Point A to Point B in a fluid manner; my pathway was to be the shortest distance between two points. It was then that I recognized we were pursuing our mutual goals in an entirely different fashion. Our mentoring experiment came to a grinding halt. She was enjoying the process, while I could only find enjoyment in accomplishing the purpose. Looking back, I now realize that she was merely being herself, and I was being myself. Neither of us was right or wrong. I was simply being a man, and she was being a woman. The grinding and polishing that takes place in a marriage often happens because of these very differences.

It is these differences between males and females that I've chosen to examine as they relate to the fine art of mentoring. In my next chapter on the unique qualities and approaches women bring to a relationship, I will offer some insights on the unique strengths and challenges women experience in mentoring. In this chapter, I want to offer some insights for men as they approach mentoring.

Like the ladies, I believe men provide some positive qualities as they participate in the art of mentoring. They incarnate certain principles that make for a rich and wonderful experience. In addition, there are also some pitfalls they will likely face. I will offer cautions to the men and then close the chapter with some practical tips they should implement.

a disclaimer

Let's begin with a simple table of the primary differences between men and women in the practice of mentoring. I recognize some of these differences are not because "men are from Mars and women from Venus" as author John Gray suggests. Some of our differences are due to style and temperament, not gender. I realize the risk I venture into as I suggest that the two sexes approach mentoring a bit differently. Please understand — I am not implying that one gender is better than the other. I'm only saying it is good to note the strengths and the challenges each gender will likely face, based on research into males and females. There are differences between men and women, and we are foolish to idealize we're all alike. The table below has two columns I call "Feelers" and "Thinkers." Research shows that women usually approach mentees as "Feelers" and men approach them as "Thinkers." When I suggest that men are usually more "thinking" creatures and women more "feeling" creatures, it doesn't mean that men don't feel and women cannot think. I'm simply underscoring the bump part of the bell curve that reveals each mentor experiences different strengths or emphases due to his or her gender. If a woman is more "thinking and result" oriented, she would profit from reading this chapter more than the next. The following two columns reveal the characteristics men and women usually embrace:

As I'll mention in the next chapter on women, we can learn from each other. Neither of these two columns is always right or wrong. Men need to adopt more of the natural female tendencies and vice versa. There should be a combination of both thinking and feeling; relationship and results; empathy and problem solving, etc. I'd like to begin with a simple list of the positive qualities men naturally bring into the mentoring experience.

FEELERS	THINKERS
Emotion	Logic
Relationships	Results
Sharing	Doing
Big Picture	Detail
Empathy	Problem Solving
Holistic	Categorical

positive qualities men possess

Although both genders own more positive characteristics than I can share in one chapter, let me zero in on five primary elements that men bring to the mentoring process.

1. *Men often enjoy getting down to business and reaching goals.*
Men don't have too much problem cutting through the fat and getting to the bottom line of what needs to happen to improve a situation. What they often need is some empathy to accompany their diagnosis and prescription for each other. Men often size up a situation and offer a number of ways to reach an objective before their mentee can say, "Do you understand my question?"

2. *Frequently, men can maintain their vision for the big picture.*
Although women are much more holistic in their perspective, they can get lost in one particular issue during a conversation. While men they think in categories, they seem to naturally be able to see each category as it relates to the "big picture." Again, they're good at seeing the "bottom line." This helps them to remain objective and solve problems for themselves and each other.

3. *Men usually have a bias for action and generally don't waste time or words.*
Have you ever heard a wife say about her husband, "He just doesn't communicate enough"? This frequently happens when the husband is stewing over a problem; he hibernates in his own world until he can think of a solution. This can be bad and good. The good component to this tendency is that men want to actually do something, not just talk about it. They will often use a few choice words and then move toward the goal.

4. *Men are often natural problem solvers.*
Clearly, this depends upon whether the subject interests them, but if it does, men will think long and hard about how to resolve any dilemma they face. If the issue is of primary concern, they can be extremely creative and offer tremendous ingenuity. Most men I know are wired with an innate interest in managing their territory (responsibilities) and their productivity (results).

5. *Men can often remain logical and objective.*
No doubt, there's a point when both genders can feel overwhelmed, and panic strikes like a snake. However, because men are often stronger at thinking than feeling, they are able to limit how much their emotions control them as they face a problem. Temperaments within both sexes will also play a role in this, but the average man usually prides himself on being logical and objective — even in a crisis.

why men struggle with relationships

Later in this handbook, I will make a case for the primacy of relationships within a healthy life. If you are a person of faith, it is especially true. Our faith should not merely be about mentally embracing creeds or doctrines. It should impact how we do relationships. Remember the two greatest commandments? The scriptures teach that we cannot separate our spiritual life (and depth) from our relationships with others.

Ironically, in our Western culture, men very often make their religion simply one category of their lives. Many don't allow their faith to impact their approach to the other categories of their lives. They may be in church on Sunday, then cuss at their employees on Monday and not even see a problem with this. Unfortunately, although men don't "do" relationships as naturally as women, they must learn to prioritize them and begin to invest in them. We simply cannot do mentoring well if we don't do relationships well.

So why don't many men do relationships well? Is it a weakness in our sexuality? Are we destined to simply be stereotypes of John Wayne or James Bond or Rambo or Tim "The Tool Man" Taylor? I don't think so. However there are some hurdles we will have to jump if we are going to excel in relationships. The following list contains some cautions that men need to be aware of, especially as they begin to mentor others. The list details why men struggle with relationships. You will notice that this list includes elements from both nature and nurture. Let's look at them before I provide you with some tips to implement.

1. *Men draw their identity more from achievement than from relationships.*
I believe one way we can summarize the differences between men and women is where they derive their primary fulfillment and identity. Women often draw their primary identity from connecting to their world; men from conquest of their world.

Men want to build, win, achieve and conquer. I realize this is a generalization — but for most, it is true. This makes stopping to do relationships well a conscious effort for them.

2. *Men are tempted to stay at their workplace where they get training and strokes.*
   Nearly every working man would say that he's received some training at his workplace. Almost the same percentage will say they've received no training whatsoever at their relationships. "Forgiveness 101" or "Listening Skills and Conflict Resolution" would be tremendously helpful courses for males but are absent from our formal training. Furthermore, because the male usually performs well at the workplace, he gets strokes from his boss, his secretary or his foreman. Conversely, when he gets home, he may get nagged, since he is not doing so well there. Men are humans. Where do you think they are tempted to linger? As this scenario emerged, so did the proverbial "workaholic."

3. *Our culture is mistaken with its masculine image.*
   In my book, *Soul Provider*, I talk about the masculine image that has prevailed in America for decades. This image can be summarized with the words: strong, silent, self-sufficient, resourceful, shrewd and, on a good day, courteous to women and to each other. This image is typified by media personalities like John Wayne, Sean Connery (James Bond), Sylvester Stallone (Rocky), Tim Allen (Tim Taylor) Brad Pitt (*Troy*) and George Clooney (*Oceans Eleven*). The images are: the cowboy, the playboy, the he-man, and the funny man. None is especially good at opening up emotionally. None is available for vulnerable and transparent accountability. Like it or not, these images have prevailed in real life as well.

4. *Men have rarely had good models of developmental relationships.*
   Few of us had patient mentors in our formative years. In addition, many of us never had fathers who knew how to be healthy leaders in our homes. This left us with little more than books on the subject. We lacked a model who demonstrated what this should look like. Due to our lack of models, men often feel like fakes when it comes to authentic leadership.

When this is true, they either compensate by simply shutting down their emotions and communication or swing to the other extreme and become overly flamboyant and demonstrative, searching for laughs or applause as an affirmation that they're OK.

5. *Men are driven to get to the bottom line and not oriented to enjoy the process.*
Still another pitfall is that men are frequently impatient when it looks like progress is not being made fast enough. We want to race to the results; we want to see the product in our hands. This tendency is fostered by our American corporate culture. Unfortunately, men must experience a paradigm shift if they are to be effective mentors. Mentoring is frequently a slow process. Mentees are shaped in a crock-pot, not a microwave oven.

6. *Men often prefer pure action over conversation.*
This is both goods news and bad news. The masculine strength is also our weakness. We want action. But, we often want it at the expense of building good, deep relationships with others. At times we'd rather not hear about someone's personal affairs if it is going to take too long and keep us from our "to do" list. Men need to learn to enjoy pure communication and conversation. That is not to say there should be no action. But results without relationship don't cut it. Men must learn to relate and identify with others.

7. *Men don't feel safe being vulnerable and revealing their feelings.*
Still another reason why relationships are difficult for men is that they don't share their honest feelings very freely. Perhaps this is because it feels so feminine to share emotions. Perhaps this is a safeguard. Women often share them too freely. Men, however, must learn to be transparent and deter- mine to build safe places to be vulnerable with a mentee or a handful of other men in an accountability group.

8. *Men want to see tangible results quickly.*
This is a second cousin to number five, above. Not only do men appear too busy to just enjoy the journey, but they also want to see visible, tangible, measurable results...fast. If they don't physically see progress, they can become discouraged, since their masculinity is driven by accomplishment.

Unfortunately, good mentoring requires close relationships, and intimacy doesn't happen overnight. Most of the time, men will have to trim back on their expectations and learn to set mini-goals. Perhaps we need to allow our mentees to make mini-decisions so that we can enjoy the process from week to week.

9. *Men can be self-sufficient.*
Finally, men must overcome their tendency to be self-reliant if they are to become effective in the relationship/mentoring business. We need to recognize that we really do need each other. Interdependence is a quality that comes naturally to most women. Men must make conscious decisions to disclose their weakness and, sometimes, even let a mentee help them. One of the best ways a man can affirm and communicate value to others is to need them and the help they can give.

some tips for men who mentor
Allow me to close this chapter by listing some practical hints that just might make you, as a male, a better mentor to others. These are based upon the insights we've just reviewed together. See what you think:

1. *Plan events together just for the sake of the relationship.*
In order to revolt against the temptation to race to the solution without relishing the journey, try planning some relational time together without discussing a deep insight or setting some lofty goal. Let your hair down, and let them see you do it. Insert a regular rhythm of these friendship times, knowing that they help you earn the right to speak into their lives.

2. *Create safe places for transparent communication.*
You may need to begin by asking for their forgiveness for your failure to model transparency and vulnerability. Once you have articulated this goal, find a place where you believe you can open up and share. Very likely, you will need to get away from the coffee shop or other public places. Write down and discuss your secret hopes, your flaws or your personal aspirations.

3. *Find models of intimacy and healthy male friendships.*
If neither of you had good models of masculine intimacy and accountability, you may want to seek out other men who exemplify this quality.

It might be good to sit down and interview this "model" together and learn side by side. Healthy relationships are more caught than taught. You need to be "exposed" to them for a season.

4. *Make healthy intimacy one of your goals.*
If you feel you fall into the category of a typical male and love setting goals for yourself, then may I suggest you make "thriving relationships" one of your goals? Set an objective for a level of intimacy and community that is measurable and achievable then pursue it with a passion. Read about it in books, listen to other men on the subject, and then discuss it together. If you want it badly enough, you'll get it. Give each other permission to be held accountable.

5. *Focus on how to capitalize on strengths.*
Men are prone to become self-reliant; they reach down into their own human reservoirs and artificially conjure up the juices to make it happen all by themselves. Because of this, we can be blind to our own strengths. We don't have an objective perspective on what we offer a relationship or a team. We need each other to see this. Maintaining a focus on the discovery of your strengths helps.

In 1987, I took my first mission trip behind the iron curtain. I led a team of young adults to serve in Budapest, Hungary. It was a marvelous experience for all of us. One of the greatest lessons I learned on that trip was the tremendous amount of labor that's involved in building a cross-cultural friendship. I had the opportunity of meeting a 19-year-old man named Adam. Developing a relationship with him was the epitome of this truth. It was work. We were two totally different people: he was from Hungary, I was from America; he was a Communist, I was a Capitalist; he spoke Hungarian, I spoke English; he was an atheist, I was a Christian. But because we were both "psyched up" to work at the relationship, it worked. We are friends to this day.

I mention this because I believe every one of us shares in cross-cultural relationships each day of our lives right here in the U.S. I am speaking of the differences between males and females. We represent two different cultures. We possess two different worldviews or perspectives; we think and feel differently, and while we may use the same words, they may mean something totally different depending on who spoke them. I guess you could say we do speak different languages! What's more, we approach the art of mentoring differently. Yet, like my friendship with Adam, if we are prepared for this and are ready to work at understanding and enjoying the differences, we can actually benefit from each other. It can be a wonderful adventure in relationships.

a disclaimer

In this chapter, I would like to communicate to you how mentoring is unique within the female gender. From my research with women and from interacting with thousands of them, I will attempt to detail the natural, positive qualities they possess that spark healthy mentoring. I'll also point out some dangers they need to guard against. Often, men and women approach people and relationships differently. They frequently embrace diverse views and have distinctive tendencies based on their sexuality. Before I begin, let me give you a disclaimer. What you are about to read are generalizations based on research. I am sure I have oversimplified both genders in my attempt to fit the information into one chapter. I am also certain that you may know of exceptions to the "rules" I will communicate. Often times, these differences between males and females statistically can simply be differences in temperament. I recognize differences between males and females can be traced back to several factors outside of gender. However, the information you'll read in this chapter is based on majority statistics — the bump part of the bell curve — and will help you better connect with the gender you are mentoring. I believe this material can help you improve 80% of the mentoring mishaps that occur as you meet with the same sex (I attempted this in the previous chapter when I address the men). Let's begin with a simple chart or table that helps put this in perspective.

The chart below outlines some differences between "Feelers" and "Thinkers." These two columns outline the differences in mentoring styles. With some exceptions, women usually approach mentees as "Feelers" and men approach them as "Thinkers." This is the Chart I introduced in the last chapter. When I say that women have a strength in "feeling" and men in "thinking", this does not mean that women don't think and men cannot feel. I am simply communicating that a natural strength for each gender — a strength they add to the other gender when they are in a relationship — is often described the words below. Let's take a look.

Obviously, we can learn from each other. Men who focus on results, for instance, don't get very far unless they learn to build relationships along the way. Women, on the other hand, can end up chatting about a struggle in their life without ever getting to the answer. Each sex compliments what the other does not possess as a strength. My goal is for us to harvest the positive elements each gender has to offer. Let's take a moment to survey the positive qualities women share as they mentor.

FEELERS	THINKERS
Emotion Relationships	Logic
Sharing	Results
Big Picture	Doing
Empathy	Detail
Holistic	Problem Solving
	Categorical

positive qualities women possess

Before we examine the cautions and struggles we must resolve, let's take a look at why women do mentoring relationships well.

1. *Women often draw their identity from the primary relationships in their lives.*
   Women naturally bond because of their innate tendency to draw identity from their connection to others. In the ancient scriptures, we read how God formed woman out of the rib of her husband, and it has forever served as a word picture of how naturally women identify with the key people in their lives.

2. *Women are often comfortable being transparent and vulnerable.*
   You usually don't have to tell women to open up and be transparent in conversation. In fact, quite the opposite is true. Women tend to draw fulfillment from their ability to share each other's pain and hardships and actually feel stronger by sharing weaknesses. Men, on the other hand, generally do not feel safe sharing their weaknesses.

3. *Women generally prioritize communication or are willing to work at it.*
   In most cases, the women I know are good at interpersonal communication. In the few cases where they are not, they have the capacity and are willing to work at it until they become effective. This is frequently not true for most men.

4. *Women are willing to be interdependent with each other.*
   Most women are not loners. They usually don't have to face the challenge of overcoming independence to the same degree as men. Women are willing to say, "I need help!" and are open to direct accountability. It does not signify failure for them just because they can't do it on their own. Making it on their own has no great appeal to women.

5. *Women are often diligent encouragers.*
This is not to say that men don't encourage each other. However, because men are often "bottom line" oriented, they may tend to offer one word of encouragement and expect the recipient to remember it for quite a while. Women don't seem to tire of offering constant words of encouragement to each other, knowing they need it themselves.

cautions for women who mentor

In order for this chapter to be genuinely helpful, we must look at the hurdles women will jump if they are to succeed at mentoring relationships. This next list represents the cautions I offer to women as they mentor:

1. *Because women can focus so strongly on bonding relationally, they can prevent themselves from reaching the results they are after.*
The emphasis on simply getting together and relating, conversing and sharing may keep women from getting to a goal in their mentoring process.

2. *Because women empathize so well, they can foster unhealthy co-dependency in which mentees look to them, exclusively, for answers.*
I have watched women in mentoring relationships create a dependence on each other that resembles a child who still needs and lives with his parents when he's a grown man. Healthy mentoring is not finished until the mentee knows how to live and lead others on her own.

3. *Because women often enjoy the details of life, they can miss the "big picture."*
It is possible for women to enter a conversation and become so engrossed with the details, sharing "verbal detours" about their day, their family, their hassles; that they lose sight of the main issue — why they've committed to meeting in the first place.

4. *Because women are so relational, they can neglect the necessary structure needed to follow through on an objective.*
Sometimes our strength is often our weakness. Females can master the relationship part of mentoring so well that they can avoid, with disdain, the very system or structure needed to keep them on track with their initial goals.

5. *Because women value relationships so highly, those relationships can be a source of comparison and competition.* Women must guard against comparing personal features, personal friendships, personal focuses and personal finesse with each other. They must remember that we will always find someone who is more beautiful, more poised socially, more talented, going a different direction and whose life appears more attractive.

6. *Because women build friendships so quickly, they can often take on too many relationships at too deep a level.* Intimacy can be invited much too quickly for many women. I have observed some who "rescue" others and become co-dependent. They soon attract so many deep relationships that they become overwhelmed. They must learn to plan ahead and establish boundaries within their relationships.

7. *Because relationships can play such an important role, the temptation exists to control them.* If held too closely, a female can be tempted to be controlling and force the direction of the relationship and how deeply it progresses.

8. *Because women tend to relate through verbal conversation, they may turn their mentoring meeting into a "chat" session that is not purpose-driven.* I believe mentoring happens best on purpose, not by accident. This means we cannot lose sight of our purpose as we meet together. Women must be conscious of the need to stay mission-driven.

some tips for women who mentor

I trust that some of these insights have been helpful. I am indebted to my wife, a godly woman and mentor to many; Nancy Hensley, who has led a number of women's groups and mentoring communities; Sheryl Fleisher, who led a large women's mentoring ministry for over a decade; Holly Moore, who is our Vice President at Growing Leaders and others who gave input on compiling these tidbits. Now that we have observed the distinctives of the female gender, examined the positive qualities they possess and surveyed the cautions they need to heed, let's close with a simple list of tips. These are practical steps I would advise most women to take to accentuate their gender gifts. These principles will help them play to their strengths and work on their weaknesses as they enter mentoring relationships:

1. *Create a set routine, rhythm and schedule for mentoring.*
   Deliberately insert structure into the relationship that will allow you to be relational, yet stay on track with where you are going. We need systems in our ministries to keep them progressing and to ensure they go beyond one generation. Plan both the time to meet and the goals to pursue.

2. *Use a "tool" for mentoring.*
   By a "tool" I simply mean a study guide or a book or some practical help that will take you where you want to go. Remember, you may be in a small community in your residence hall or a small group ministry in your church and not do anything but "hang out" each week. In a mentoring relationship, by definition, you want to reach your potential, not just fellowship. Select a mentoring tool that will help you reach the specific goals you set.

3. *Keep the end in mind and the goal before your eyes.*
   Since you do relationships naturally, you won't need to work as hard on that component of mentoring. Instead you will need to remind each other of the goals you've set and even maintain a list of the objectives in front of you at each meeting.

4. *Work together to reinforce your identity based on your unique strengths and wiring.*
   Your identity does not come from comparing yourself to other women, even when that may be a natural temptation. You must hold each other accountable to reinforce where your identity should be drawn from — who you were born to be.

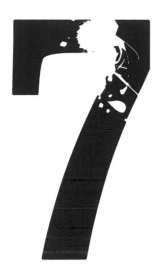

It was wise advice when someone once said: "Everyone needs a mentor, including mentors."

Each of us should always be looking to someone who is a step ahead of us in life; someone who helps us examine our habits, our schedules, our thoughts, our feelings, our strengths and our results. This chapter will address how to find such a person, whatever your age or stage in life.

recognize what you are looking for

As you seek a mentor, you must understand what it is you are looking for, or you may not recognize them when you meet them. Keep in mind, mentors are not..

- perfect people.
- leaders who try to make you look and act like them.
- workers who want to use you to help accomplish their goals.
- people who give you time out of duty and obligation.
- successes who will give you a "free ride" to fame and fortune.

Instead, mentors are humans, just like you, who are further along in life (maturity) and have chosen to make "deposits" in others. Mentors are genuine, giving, caring, insightful and secure people. Author Bobb Biehl once said:

- MENTORS are more like caring aunts and uncles than like another mother or father.

- MENTORS are those with whom we share the lows and celebrate the highs in life... together!
- MENTORS are those rare individuals in life who love us deeply... see our greatest potentials... cheer us on... correct when needed... teach us selflessly about life... become our lifelong friends... at whose funerals we weep unashamedly... with no regard whatsoever for the clock.

It is my hope that every person who reads this handbook finds such a person. In order for that to happen, you must take some initial steps.

taking the first step

Often I encourage a young adult to seek out a mentor. When I do, that young adult is frequently convinced that there are none anywhere near them. They claim their school or workplace or church has no one with any internal depth or with any time. They contend their town is too small, or the generation gap is too wide to connect with someone closely. There are simply none to be found.

In such a case, I generally recommend that the young adult open their minds to a mentor who might look very different than their stereotype. In my own journey, I'm constantly amazed at the help I find when I become open to mentors outside of my narrow assumptions about how they should look. I am frequently surprised with an answer right under my nose. This has happened dozens of times in my life. I have been mentored by engineers, homemakers, accountants, authors, business executives, publishers, pastors and financial advisors. You, too, may be amazed to find that a potential mentor already exists nearby, but you didn't have the "eyes" to see them. Perhaps you're looking for an ideal mentor that truly doesn't exist... anywhere in the world. Sometimes, you must take what you can get.

Second, be willing to sacrifice to find them. This may mean driving a couple of hours to meet with them each month. It could mean you are to meet with someone each month face to face and to add a second or third person that you correspond with via email or Facebook or even texting, who adds some dimensions to the mentoring that the face-to-face person doesn't possess. Right now, I have two mentors I meet with over the phone on a regular basis. That's fine, too.

Third, be open to the idea that a perfect mentor doesn't exist, but you might find a perfect mentoring experience among several mentors. Each year, I choose five or six categories in which I want to grow that year.

They may be issues such as becoming a better leader, a better dad, a better financial investor, a better communicator or whatever. Then, I choose individuals who can be mentors for those individual categories. In other words, I don't expect one person to become a guru like Socrates or Moses. I allow people to mentor me in a single issue. It becomes a win/win because they feel comfortable with that expectation.

Finally, keep your antennas up. Everywhere you go in your daily routines, be on the lookout for potential mentors. Stay conscious of the value that each person you meet adds to your life. Mentors are everywhere if you just stop and think about it.

choosing a mentor

When you are ready to approach a potential mentor, be ready to do most of the work. Dr. Ted Engstrom recommends that you keep the following list in mind.

1. Ask him or her to help you ask the right questions, search in the right places and stay interested in the right answers.

2. Decide what degree of excellence or perfection you want. Generally the goal of mentoring is improvement, not perfection. Perhaps only a few can be truly excellent, but all can become better.

3. Accept a subordinate, learning position. Don't let ego get in the way of learning, and don't try to impress the mentor with your knowledge or ability and, consequently, set up a mental barrier against taking in as fast as it's being given out.

4. Respect the mentor but don't idolize him. Respect allows us to accept what he or she is teaching, but making the mentor an idol removes our critical faculty for fitting a mentor's thinking to ourselves.

5. Put into effect immediately what you are learning. The best mentoring is intensity in a narrow field. Learn, practice and assimilate.

55

6. Set up a discipline for relating to the mentor. Arrange for an ample and consistent time schedule, select the subject matter in advance and do your homework to make the sessions profitable.

7. Reward your mentor with your own progress. If you show appreciation but make no progress, the mentor knows he or she has failed. Your progress is his highest reward.

8. Learn to ask crucial questions — questions that prove you have been thinking between sessions; questions that show progress in your perception.

9. Don't threaten to give up. Let your mentor know that you have made a decision for progress; that he is dealing with a persistent person; a determined winner. Then he knows he is not wasting his time.

set your goals

I always recommend that the first ingredient you look for in a mentor is that they model excellence in character and in some area in which you wish to grow. I have consistently tried to find leaders of great character — those who exemplify integrity and trustworthiness. If a mentee is going to be a mirror reflection of his mentor, I better choose them wisely.

The second ingredient a mentor should look for in a mentor is strength in the area in which they wish to grow. Mentees should first spot an area of expertise or mastery in that person that qualifies them to speak on the issue with authority and credibility. For example, all six of my mentors have natural strengths in the areas for which I've asked them to mentor me. I can learn most from them in those areas. Their strength should match your desire and become your focus, as a mentee.

I recommend your mentoring experience should reflect the 70-25-5 Rule:

1. Spend 70% of your time developing your strengths.
2. Spend 25% of your time on areas in which you wish to grow.
3. Spend 5% of your time on areas of weakness.

Over the last several years I've attempted to match up hundreds of people in mentoring relationships. Because the college students with whom I have worked varied so greatly in their maturity and interests, I came up with a simple formula to help them all find a suitable mentor. You might say I crystallized the bare essentials of a mentor; I reduced the criteria to the lowest common denominator. It became the goal for each student who sought a mentor. Interestingly, the elements actually spell the word GOALS:

G- *GENEROSITY* – They must be willing to give generously of their time, resources and wisdom. They see their mentee as an important part of their world.

O- *OBJECTIVITY* – They must be able to see strengths and weaknesses clearly and be willing to communicate those honestly.

A- *AUTHENTICITY* – They must be real. You must be able to see their humanity; they should be genuine, transparent and open with you.

L- *LOYALTY* – They must be people who are loyal to others. When friendships (or mentoring relationships) are formed, they are committed to them.

S- *STRENGTH* – They must possess a strength in an area you are interested in; one in which you wish to grow and mature.

Why not set out on your pursuit of a mentor with this "blueprint" in mind? You will probably find that potential mentors possess several other qualities that will enrich your life, but these five lay a great foundation for producing a healthy relationship.

Remember: Seeking out mentors is ancient wisdom. King Solomon encouraged it thousands of years ago in his proverbs from ancient Israel. The following are some of his insights paraphrased from his writings:

> Counsel in another heart is like deep water,
> but a discerning man will draw it up.
> *(Proverbs 20:5)*
>
> A straightforward answer is as good as a kiss of friendship.
> *(Proverbs 24:26)*
>
> As iron sharpens iron, so one man sharpens the wit of another.
> *(Proverbs 27:17)*

57

a checklist

To conclude this chapter I want to provide a checklist for finding and choosing a mentor:

- Will the mentor be an objective, lovingly honest and balanced source of feedback for your questions?
- Will the mentor be open and transparent with their own struggles?
- Will the mentor model their teachings?
- Does the mentor know and believe in you...one of your chief cheerleaders and not your chief critic?
- Will the mentor teach as well as answer your questions?
- Is the mentor successful in your eyes?
- Will the mentor be open to two-way communication... learning from you on occasion as well as teaching you?
- Does the mentor want to see younger people succeed in developing their spiritual and leadership potential?

A final note: Refer to the "Mentor Match-up" form I provide in Chapter 19. This helpful little profile will enable you to locate the appropriate mentor or mentee that fits your personality, style and goals.

When you are ready to invest your life in someone else, the first question you'll face is: WHO? In whom should I regularly make deposits? How will I know if I've chosen someone wisely? Is there some kind of guideline that can help me make this decision?

In the next few pages, I'll attempt to outline the answers to these questions. I believe we ought to seek what we'll call a "divine appointment," as a first step when it comes to our mentee. Keep your antennas up for the right person to cross your path. Some of my most productive mentoring relationships have been serendipitous; they came out of simply doing life and finding someone in my path. However, while this will happen, there are some wisdom principles that we can employ in our decision.

you must look for faith

Over the last thirty years I've mentored hundreds of college students, interns and young professionals who committed time to mentoring relationship or our internship program at Growing Leaders and the other organizations in which I have served. The inner qualities I looked for in potential interns (mentees) can be summarized in the acrostic: FAITH.

F- *FAITHFUL*
Is this person faithful to commitments they've made, as well as to the disciplines of personal growth?

A- *AVAILABLE*
Does this person have the time, and do they make themselves available to growth opportunities as a priority?

I- *INITIATIVE*
Do they show initiative in their desire to grow? Are they willing to take the first step without someone "holding their hand?"

T- *TEACHABLE*
Is this person willing to learn new truths and be open to change? Do they exhibit a "soft" or a stubborn heart? Will they learn from you?

H- *HUNGRY*
Does this person have a passion to grow and reach their potential? Do they hunger for to stretch and grow?

If you can find a person who meets each of these criteria, it will be difficult to make a bad decision. Memorize the FAITH acrostic and keep the questions in mind.

mentoring potential leaders
If you're committed to mentoring potential leaders, those who'll influence people and organizations, you may want to include an additional acrostic in your criteria: GIFTS:

G- *GIFTED*
Do they exhibit some obvious gifts for leadership? Do they have the aptitude and potential? Are they good communicators, organizers, planners or strategizers?

I- *INFLUENCIAL*
Are they already influencing their peers and the groups with whom they associate? Do they have social capital? Even without a title, do they leave their mark on others?

F- *FRUITFUL*
When they set their hand to do something, do they get results? Do they get the job done? They should be people who don't need an official position to produce.

T- *TRUSTWORTHY*
Do they seem credible with their life and leadership? With all the gifts they have, is their character as deep as their gifts? Can they be trusted with responsibility?

S- *SERVING*
Are they already serving in some capacity? Are they actively involved in the community, proving they have a heart to serve and make a difference?

the bottom line
The bottom line is this: You want to pursue mentees that demonstrate they are ready for what you have to offer. Certainly, some young people mature at slower rates than others. I am not suggesting you only seek out the next Bill Gates or Mark Zuckerburg or Steve Jobs. I am only saying, choose someone that won't frustrate you because they are flaky in their commitments and unproven as to their readiness. In short, it can all be summarize in three words. You want to find:

1. *APTITUDE*
   Do they exhibit an aptitude for leadership? Are they good thinkers? Do they reflect and act strategically when they get involved? Do they want to do something with their life? Are they going somewhere in their future?

2. *RELIABILITY*
   Do you consider them to be reliable with any instruction or request they receive? Do they show a faithful spirit to the things they already know to do? Are they mature enough to demonstrate they will appreciate and act on the time and effort you invest?

3. *POTENTIAL*
   Are they high-potential people? Can you see a vision for them and a passion to impact others in their world? Do you feel certain they will reproduce what you give them? Even if they are still rough around the edges, do you see a glimmer of hope for their potential?

QUESTION:
do you know anyone who fits this criteria?

factors in your relationship

Paul Stanley reminds us of an additional component to the decision: "Mentoring is an empowering experience that requires a connection between two people...the mentor and the mentee. Factors such as time, proximity, needs, shared values and goals affect any relationship. But the mentoring relationship needs three additional factors, or dynamics, to bring about empowerment. These dynamics are constantly at play in the context of a mentoring relationship and directly affect the mentee's progress, change and level of empowerment."

The following dynamics are vital to the mentoring relationship:

1. *Attraction* — This is the necessary starting point in the mentoring relationship. The mentee is drawn to the mentor for various reasons: perspective, certain skills, experience, value and commitments modeled, perceived wisdom, position, character, knowledge and influence. The mentor is attracted to the mentee's attitude, potential and opportunity for influence. As attraction increases, trust, confidence and mentoring subjects develop that will strengthen the mentoring relationship and ensure empowerment.

2. *Responsiveness* — The mentee must be willing and ready to learn from the mentor. Attitude is crucial for the mentee. A responsive, receiving spirit on the part of the mentee and attentiveness on the part of the mentor directly speed up and enhance the empowerment.

3. *Accountability* — Mutual responsibility for one another in the mentoring process ensures progress and closure. Sharing expectations and a periodic review and evaluation will give strength to application and facilitate empowerment. The mentor should take responsibility for initiating and maintaining accountability with the mentee.

The more deliberate and intense the mentoring relationship, the more important these dynamics are. Why is this true? Because mutual commitment fosters change and growth to take place. These dynamics are the ingredients that produce this commitment.

Because of these dynamics, the selection of your mentee becomes a crucial decision. Please make it carefully. Doctors tell us the most formative years of growth are ages 1-5.

The second most formative are ages 20-25. A brain is taking shape the first three decades of life. Your deposits in a young mind could shape their values and change the trajectory of their life. We must choose those individuals intentionally.

common questions on mentoring

Gleaning from the wisdom of such men as Ted Engstrom, Bobb Biehl, Howard Hendricks, John Maxwell, Robert Clinton and Paul Stanley, the following list of questions and answers are provided for your benefit. Read them over carefully.

1. *Where does mentoring happen?*
   Everywhere. Most mentoring takes place in a very relaxed setting as it did centuries ago in fatherly apprenticeships. It can happen while walking, sailing, golfing, driving... anywhere you are with your mentor or your mentee. Mentoring often happens ten minutes at a time...here and there as you move through life together. Don't see mentoring as all work. It often involves the joy of mutual sharing. Mentoring happens more in the context of a relationship than a formal classroom. Mentoring is a life attitude as much as a formal structure. It can be even more enjoyable as you are doing things you enjoy together!

2. *At what age do you want to begin mentoring someone?*
   At the age where they have clear goals they want to reach. This may begin around age 16 or, in some situations, even a little earlier.

3. *What difference does age play in the mentoring process?*
   Age is not as large a factor as experience and maturity. Sometimes the mentor is actually a few years younger than the protégé. However, if you were to take all of the mentors in the world, I'd estimate that most would be between 5-20 years older than the mentees.

4. *What happens when a mentee or mentor fails?*
   No mentee wants to fail, but sometimes they need a mentor's help to know how to succeed... and how to learn from failure. A wise mentor expects a mentee to be less than perfect, especially in the formative years. A mentee should have NO FEAR OF BEING REJECTED by the mentor. It is also helpful for the mentor and mentee to discuss failure, including the freedom to fail and not be rejected before the inevitable failure occurs. No mentor wants to fail.

A wise mentee expects a mentor to be less than perfect. A mentor should also have NO FEAR OF BEING REJECTED by the mentee.

5. *Does a mentor have to be an ideal model of success?*
No...no mentor is perfect! Each mentor only needs to be stronger in some areas than the mentee in order to be a big help. At the same time, if the mentor has a major problem, it is difficult to lead a mentee in this area. That is why, ideally, each mentor also has one or more mentors.

6. *What effect does a mentee's motivation level have on a mentor?*
The more eager a mentee is to learn, the more eager the mentor is to teach! There is an old saying: When the student is ready, the teacher will appear. This simply means that a student's passion to learn will cause wisdom to surface from many places.

7. *Can a man mentor a woman or a woman mentor a man?*
Most studies indicate that in business today, many men mentor both men and women. At the same time, many women mentor both genders. However, mixing genders can be distracting and dangerous. I tend to encourage same-gender mentoring, challenging older women to help younger women and for older men to help younger men. Because the relationship between the mentor and the mentee typically becomes emotionally intimate, it is POTENTIALLY very dangerous to share this with the opposite sex outside of marriage. I do not recommend it.

Some mentors tell me they are forced to mentor the opposite sex because there is no one else of the same gender to take on the task. Perhaps it is a male leader who has some sharp female students or a female leader who oversees some potential male leaders, and they long for a mentor to help them. This is a tough situation.

If you must enter into a mixed gender mentoring relationship, I suggest you create a mentoring community with both females and males in it. That way, it is a safe group for both genders to share and it is less likely to have any sexual or emotional affair to occur. When the mentoring experience is complete, look to one of the graduates to take on a group themselves to mentor the same gender.

8. *What role does accountability play in the mentor/mentee relationship?*
The main reason for accountability is to help mentees reach vocational, emotional, intellectual or spiritual maturity and to develop their full leadership potential. Mentors must hold the mentees accountable, not on a daily or weekly basis, but as needed and agreed upon. The frequency and level of accountability will vary with each mentee.

Mentors are not accountable for the success of their mentees. Mentors can help mentees succeed in reaching their goals... but the responsibility for reaching goals always remains clear with the mentees. Mentors are responsible TO their mentees, but not FOR them.

9. *How confident do most people feel about becoming mentors?*
Most of the adults I have met feel somewhat intimidated by the word MENTORING. However, most people do not realize how effective they could be. Their fears prevent them from seeing their possibilities. If the word is intimidating, don't use it. Use another word like "coaching" or meeting for the purpose of growth.

At the same time, most adults can quickly name three young people who could benefit from their support and encouragement. Most people say they would have benefited from such a supportive relationship in their life or, in fact, did while they were younger. Whatever you do, don't let a little discomfort keep you from approaching one to three high potential young people and offering your mentoring support. They need your experience, wisdom and encouragement!

10. *What difference does mentoring make over a lifetime?*
Mentoring can make an extremely significant difference in a leader's lifetime achievements. Often one timely idea or a single word of encouragement influences a young leader to hang in there. One simple cup-of-coffee conversation at a critical time may shape a young leader's entire life direction. Wisely shared perspective can build faith, sustain courage and lead to visionary change and powerful accomplishments.

Many suicide notes say something like, "When I needed help, no one seemed to care about me personally... I was all alone... no one cares if I live or die!"

As rare as physical suicide may be, emotional, spiritual, family and career suicides are quite common. However, with a mentor in place who loves the mentee, this is rarely the case. Therefore, in some situations mentoring is actually the critical link to life.

Ask yourself this simple question: "What difference would a sharp, caring mentor have made in my life at an early age?" What if someone had approached you and said, "I really believe in you. In fact, I care about you so much, I'd like to meet with you and do everything in my power to make sure you succeed at your goals. I am going to ask you two simple questions each meeting: 'What are your priorities?' and 'How can I help?' I think your life is going to make a difference in the world, and I want to help empower you to reach your potential!" Now don't you think that would have made a difference in what you attempted as a young adult?

11. *Does a mentor/mentee relationship last for a lifetime?*
Ideally yes! But realistically...seldom. It is best to agree upon a set time (six months to a year) and then evaluate. At that point you can decide whether to stop or continue.

Occasionally the relationship changes as the mentor moves away. Occasionally the relationship changes as the needs of the mentee change in different life phases. Occasionally conflict arises and the relationship simply stops. Most typically, the mentoring friendship lasts a lifetime.

12. *What happens when the mentee outgrows the mentor?*
Frequently, great pain comes into the mentor and mentee relationship when a mentee outgrows their mentor. A broken relationship often occurs. When this happens, the mentee must be sure to not burn any bridges. Show gratitude for the past and allow the mentor to respond however they must. The mentee must not feel responsible for the feelings of the mentor. Ideally, the relationship should change from mentor/mentee to a friendship. Mentors should be honored to see their mentees succeed — much as fathers and mothers are honored by the success of their children in adulthood. Mentors must be secure in their own identity for this to occur.

13. *What if my mentor or mentee doesn't follow through with our initial agreement?*
First of all, STAY POSITIVE. Assume the best; that a mentor or mentee wants to get together but is just busy. Take the initiative. Don't wait and let your fears and anxiety build. Probably just a difference of assumptions or a busy schedule is the problem, not a personal reason. In your relationship with your mentee/mentor, always take the high road. You are not being rejected! Keep your mentor (or mentee) informed. Communication is of utmost importance. I learned years ago that people are down on what they are not up on.

We tend to get negative and assume the worst unless we communicate.

You may need to redefine your relationship to require less time or a different time that is better for both of your schedules. Don't give up; just redefine.

a checklist
It's wise to have in mind the kind of mentee you're looking for before you begin searching for one. The following is a checklist to help you make a decision. Does the potential mentee possess these qualities?

- Will you be able to believe 100% in this person?
- Do you naturally enjoy communicating with this person?
- Will you be able to give without reservation to this person?
- Will you love him or her like a brother or sister (family member)?
- Do you admire their potential as a leader?
- Does this person admire you?
- Is this person self-motivated even though not always confident?
- Will this person be threatened by you or threatening to you?
- Does this person have the time to meet regularly?
- Is this person teachable...eager to learn and mature in his leadership potential?

steps to effective mentoring
1. Select a mentee whose philosophy of life you share. Our greatest mentors are those who are also our models and values.

2. Choose a person with potential you genuinely believe in. Some of the nation's greatest athletes have come from tiny schools that receive no publicity. All those ball players needed was for scouts to recognize the potential that great coaching could bring out. The secret of mentoring in any field is to help a person get to where he or she is willing to go.

3. Evaluate a mentee's progress constantly. An honest mentor will be objective. If necessary, he or she will encourage the mentee to stay on course, to seek another direction or even to enter into a relationship with another mentor.

4. Be committed, serious and available to mentees. New York Philharmonic Conductor Zubin Mehta said of a young pianist: "I cannot teach him how to play, for he knows what the composer wanted to say; I can simply help him say it."

a final note

Please refer to the "Mentor Match-up" form in Appendix B to use as a guide for your decision.

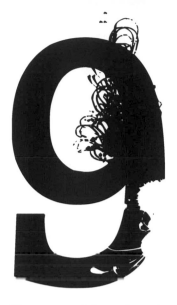

The more I travel and speak on this subject, the more I'm discovering how new it is to most people. It's not so much that the idea is new, but to actually practice developmental relationships is rare, indeed. We talk about mentoring more readily than we do it. For many, the idea of mentoring is vogue, but it's also still vague.

Most adults I meet (even professionals) still feel like they need to be mentored. Regardless of their age, gender, marital status, vocation or experience, the majority of the folks I come in contact with perceive themselves to be a "person in need" looking for a "guru." I recently spoke in New York and met a sharp gentleman I guessed to be about 65 years old. He had participated in community events all his life, had served on almost every committee imaginable and had been a leader in his town and his church for as long as he could remember. Yet as we interacted following our event, I saw a hunger in his eyes for what I had spoken about; he was crying out for a mentor! He asked me what I thought he should do. I thought for sure he meant he was looking for someone to mentor, but alas, I misunderstood him. He was in search of a mentor.

I'm not sure if my answer provided much comfort for him. I told him I would be on the lookout for appropriate mentor(s) to come beside him. I also reminded him to discard the notion that one "perfect" mentor would come along and eliminate his quest for answers. In fact, most often our answers come through the voices of several mentors, some of whom might be right under our noses, while others might live far away and require phone conversations.

Once again, we need to be open to redefine our stereotypes of mentors.

Following our conversation, I added these words, which I direct to you as well: Whatever you do possess, pass it on now! In other words, if we wait to be mentored before we feel equipped to multiply, we'll never get around to mentoring someone else! We will produce still one more generation fumbling through life in the dark! Yes, I admit it's pitiful that so many of us in our generation have never been mentored, and yes, I agree we should be looking for that mentor as we progress through our journey as adults. But, I fear that if we don't go ahead and give away the gifts we already have in our possession — via a mentoring relationship — we will reproduce another empty, disconnected, wounded and disappointed generation of people graduating from our schools and leading our nation.

I love the story of the elderly gentleman who boarded a bus with a bouquet of flowers in his hand. As he sat down, he noticed an attractive young girl sitting across from him. Her eyes kept drifting over to the flowers. It was obvious that she was taken by them. In a few minutes it was time for the man to get off the bus. Standing to his feet, he handed the flowers to the girl and said, "I noticed that you like flowers. I would like for you to have these. I think my wife would like for you to have them, too. I'll tell her I gave them to you." With that, he stepped off the bus... and entered the gate of a small cemetery.

The beauty of the story is that the man gave the "gift" he had to someone who could use and appreciate it. Rather than dwelling on the past, he invested in the future. Gandhi, the famous Indian revolutionary, would have agreed with that gentleman's logic. One day, while boarding a train in India, he lost one of his sandals. As it tumbled to the tracks, Gandhi attempted to reach it but failed. At that point, he did a strange thing. He removed his other sandal and tossed it on to the track next to the first one. When his fellow passengers asked him why he'd done it, he simply replied, "When some poor fellow finds that first sandal, now he'll have a pair he can wear."

how do i approach a potential mentoring relationship?
Do you ever wonder how to ask someone to enter a mentoring relationship with you? For many, it is best to throw away the term "mentor."

It's just too intimidating. Instead, make it natural. Take a moment and learn from the best mentors in history. Think about Socrates or Plato. Consider Confucius.

Each of these men provides insights on selecting mentees. Socrates, for instance, would spend time in Greek bath houses, just like we might spend time at a fitness center today. It was a place to meet people socially. He would enjoy striking up conversations — even debates — with other men, just to see how intellectually sharp others were. These debates often led to a mentoring relationship.

Personally, I'm frequently struck by the simplicity of how Jesus selected his twelve disciples (or mentees). Whatever you conclude about his identity, he provides an amazing case study for us to learn from today. It appears that He simply prayed all night, and then chose a handful of men — from scratch! What's more, it seems as though they just up and left their work to follow Him, without any prior knowledge of what they were in for. Oh, if it were only that easy today, we sigh. If only we could find a mentor with that much authority and credibility, or, if only we could get people to follow our mentoring that quickly.

Upon closer study we discover that it really wasn't that easy. Let's learn from both the model of Socrates and Jesus and use them as case studies on how to select mentees. No doubt, there was a time when both did issue a challenge to their "disciples," and the mentees did, indeed, follow. I do not believe, however, that this was their first exposure to Socrates or Jesus. I believe there was a PROCESS involved that required several stages of relationship. My good friend Steve Moore and I have assigned titles to these stages of relationships to help you see the process necessary for people to make the kind of commitment that mentoring requires. I share this with you to liberate you from unrealistic expectations and to give you a path to take as you enter the process yourself. Let me outline these stages as a case study for you to examine.

come and see...

This is stage one. For Socrates, it began with his walks through Athens or his conversations with other men in the bathhouse. He would engage potential mentees and screen them in or out to see if they were hungry to learn. It was a simple first encounter to spot chemistry and curiosity. For Jesus, stage one began when He discovers that two men are following Him.

71

He asks them what they are seeking. They inquire where He is staying. They are obviously at a curiosity level. They just want to know a little bit more about Him and what it means to be associated with Him. After all, He was intriguing. His response is simply: "Come and see."

For us, this may mean offering an opportunity to a potential mentee to join us in some community service, or observe some task in action or to have coffee with us — just to get acquainted. If you are going to win their trust, you need to give them time. By offering these opportunities, you are demonstrating first your commitment and intentions to them. The curiosity level is low, and the challenge is simple and easy. Your relationship may even be in its early stages. Your appropriate call on their life is simply: come and see.

come and follow...

This is stage two. At this point, Socrates would sit with a group of men and begin laying out some deep philosophy he had been pondering. It was often so deep and profound that many would simply walk away. Socrates expected this. He was putting his potential students through a filter. One day, his discourse continued for hours, and when he looked up, only Plato remained with him. Jesus did something similar. At this stage, He believed His disciples were ready to actually make a commitment and follow after Him as a mentor. At first, Simon Peter hesitated, but Jesus knew he was ready for stage two. He simply said to this fisherman: "Do not fear, from now on you will be catching men." These kinds of words are to be spoken to those ready for the commitment level; those who are ready to sacrifice in order to go forward and grow further. The word "follow" means "repeated, deliberate steps." Everyone is not ready for this level of commitment to a mentoring process. At this stage, mentees prove themselves to be faithful to the routines, the little tasks and the assignments given by the mentor. These routines might be faithfulness in meeting together, reading books that you'll later discuss together, performing a task, keeping a journal, etc. At this stage, the mentee is clearly prepared to deliberately follow the mentor.

come and surrender...

This is stage three. Socrates would further screen his mentees by providing deeper intellectual stimulus or by posing a larger question for them to ponder. It was a way for his students to demonstrate their deep convictions about his philosophy.

Somewhere in the midst of Jesus's three-and-a-half year period with the twelve, He also issued a deeper challenge to them as mentees. You might say He asked them to "surrender"; to make the ultimate commitment. He said: "If anyone wishes to come after Me, let him deny himself, take up his cross and follow Me." Of course, none of us literally ask for this kind of commitment, but it illustrates a new level.

This level of challenge is appropriate for those at the conviction level. If a person is ready to take this deep and heavy step, it will become clear by their reaction. It will also be clear if they are not. Jesus asked a wealthy, young synagogue ruler to sell everything he had (something He did not ask of everyone He met) and to come follow Him. The young man, who assumed he was further along in his spiritual maturation than he was, just dropped his head and walked away. The step was too big for him to take.

At this stage, the mentee has so bought into the mentor that they not only love the mentor but their cause as well. Profound steps of action can be expected from the mentee because the maturity level is deep. It is very appropriate, then, to issue a challenge: come and surrender.

come and multiply...

This is the fourth stage. Socrates was not as intentional about this stage as Jesus was. Plato certainly reproduced himself as a mentor, but multiplication was not for every mentee. This is where Socrates and Jesus differ. During the latter part of Jesus's mentoring relationship with the twelve, He began to send them out to mentor others themselves. In fact, the final words He spoke to them are called "the Great Commission": "Go and make disciples of all nations... teaching them to obey all that I've commanded you..." They were to duplicate what He had just done with them as mentees. This is the commissioned level. They were to go full circle – all of them. At this point, the mentee is ready to become a mentor. If they are to continue stretching and growing, they must be "pushed out of the nest" and made to fly. They must pass on what they've received; they must imitate the process and duplicate the lifestyle. Unfortunately, very few ever reach this level. Many stop and are satisfied at merely being mentored. Perhaps this is why Jesus reminded His mentees: "Freely you have received, freely give."

what is supposed to happen in a mentoring relationship?

So what is it we are called to do if we mentor someone else? Good question. Over the last several years I have made it my aim to distill the ingredients that make a good mentoring experience. The following word pictures represent what I believe are the most helpful goals you can shoot for as you attempt to invest in someone.

1. *Paint Pictures*

   Pictures stick longer than mere words. Your mentee likely grew up in the digital generation with MTV, photographs, videos, DVDs and movies. There are screens everywhere and images abound. I believe the surest way to deliver a memorable message is to paint a picture in their mind. Use metaphors, images, word pictures and stories to drive home the principle you want them to catch. I try to live by the axiom: Give them a point for their head and a picture for their heart.

2. *Give "Handles"*

   Everyone possesses some knowledge of truth. Most people, however, are hard pressed to own it in such a way as to use it in everyday life. Simply put, "handles" are things we can grab on to. Every door has a handle; every drawer has a handle. We give people "handles" when we summarize truths or principles in a user-friendly fashion so they can wrap their arms around it. Truth becomes a principle they can live by. When someone has a "handle" on something, it means they "own it" and can practice it as well as communicate it to others. A good mentor can distill or crystallize truth so that the complex becomes simple.

   For instance mentors may provide a "handle" for their mentees by summarizing the truth they are discussing into a brief phrase, slogan, metaphor or jingle. They may choose to add a memorable experience together. An example for service may be working in a soup kitchen or serving in a retirement home.

3. *Offer "Roadmaps"*

   Roadmaps give us direction in our journey and a view of the "big picture." When we give someone a "roadmap," we are passing on a life compass to them. In the same way that maps help us travel on roads we've never been on, these life roadmaps show us where we are; they help people not only to see the right road but to see that road in relation to all the other roads. They also help a person stay off the wrong roads.

They provide perspective on the whole picture. This generally happens only when we communicate intentionally, not accidentally. While there is a place for spontaneous interaction, planned opportunities to speak into a mentee's life are necessary. Friendship may happen by chance, mentoring happens on purpose. Roadmaps help mentees navigate their way through life.

4. *Provide "Laboratories"*
When we provide "laboratories" for our mentees, we are giving them a place to practice the principles we've discussed with them. Do you remember science class in college? Science always included a lecture and a "lab." By definition, laboratories are safe places in which to experiment. We all need a "lab" to accompany all the "lectures" we get in life. In these "labs," we learn the right questions to ask, the appropriate exercises to practice, an understanding of the issues and experiential knowledge of what our agenda should be in life. Good laboratories are measurable: They have a beginning and an ending point, they can be evaluated together, and they provide ideas for life application. In these labs, mentors can supervise their mentees like a coach. They can oversee their experimentation like a professor. They can interpret life like a parent. Every time I meet with my mentees, I have a "laboratory" idea to accompany the principle I want them to learn. This forces me to be creative, but I believe in the axiom: Information without application leads to intellectual constipation!

5. *Furnish "Roots"*
One of the most crucial goals mentors ought to have for their mentees is to give them "roots and wings." This popular phrase describes everyone's need for foundations to be laid and for the freedom to soar and broaden their horizons. The foundation we must help to lay in our mentees involves the construction of a "character-based life" versus an "emotion-based life." This means we help them develop core values to live by. They should leave us possessing strong convictions by which they can live their lives and the self-esteem to stand behind those convictions. The deeper the roots, the taller a tree can grow and the more durable that tree is during a storm. If you are training someone for a service industry, don't move on to heavy and glamorous subjects with them until they've mastered the basics and have deep roots.

6. *Supply "Wings"*
The final word picture that describes what a mentor must give a mentee is "wings." We give someone wings when we enable them to think big and expect big things from life and from themselves. When someone possesses wings, they are free to explore and to plumb the depths of their own potential. When mentors give wings, they help mentees soar to new heights in their future.

Consequently, it's as important to teach them how to ask questions as how to obtain answers. Mentors should empower mentees to take the limits off what they might accomplish with their lives and be filled with joy when their mentees surpass their own level of personal achievement.

Dr. Howard Hendricks remembers a professor he had in college who continued to study and consume books late into his life. When he asked his "prof" why he spent so much time pouring over his books, the instructor responded simply: "It is because I'd rather my students drink from a flowing stream than a stagnant pool."

This is the kind of mindset that fosters healthy and hungry mentees. When we provide handles, roadmaps, laboratories, roots and wings, we spawn strong, growing leaders who are healthy and effective. The ingredients of "grace and truth" take on new meaning. This is what empowers mentees: grace and truth. Grace is the relational love that knows no conditions; it is the warm, personal side of mentoring. Truth is the firm, steady, objective guide that provides a stable foundation for life. In other words mentors have a compass in their heads and a magnet in their hearts.

Deanna was a high school student who always made good grades — until she took chemistry. Somehow she just didn't get it, no matter how hard she tried. As a matter of fact, she ended up failing the course. Fortunately, her teacher was also her mentor. He knew how devastating it would be to Deanna and her family to see an "F" on her report card. Still, he had to give her the grade. He vacillated over how to deal with the situation. Finally, he found the answer by offering both grace and truth. On her report card, he simply put an "F" next to the subject of Chemistry. However, on the same line he wrote these words: "We cannot all be chemists...but oh, how we would all love to be Deanna's."

the seven gifts of a mentor

All of us need mentors who can give the gift of grace and truth. We are not fully empowered when we receive one without the other.

Over the years I have tried to put in a nutshell the "gifts" that good mentors give to mentees. While every mentoring relationship is unique, I believe there are certain universal resources that can be passed on if a mentor wants to invest in someone. Frequently, I will hear someone say: "I have never been in a formal mentoring relationship."

What exactly is supposed to transpire when we meet? Is there an optimal format to follow? What sort of exchange should happen between mentor and mentee?

The answer to these questions may vary. There is no one right thing to say or do when you meet with your mentee. I suppose the one common non-negotiable that every good mentor shares is this: They modeled what they taught. They didn't just say it; they lived it. They practiced what they preached.

In addition to this essential ingredient, I have listed the God-given resources that I believe every good mentor should impart to their mentee over time. If you are just beginning this process, this list should be especially helpful to you. The following list represents seven categories that provide a guideline as you think through what could and should happen on a regular basis.

The Seven Gifts a Mentor Gives

1. *ACCOUNTABILITY*......This involves holding a person to the commitments they have made. It may involve bringing a list of tough questions to the meeting and asking your mentee to respond honestly to them.

2. *AFFIRMATION*......This involves speaking words of encouragement, love and support to your mentee, affirming their strengths, their thoughts, their actions and their service.

3. *ASSESSMENT*......This involves objectively evaluating their present state and giving them an assessment on what you see; it enables them to gain perspective from an outside point of view.

4. *ADVICE*......This involves speaking words of wise counsel and giving them options for their decisions. It means providing direction and navigation for their life.

5. *ADMONISHMENT*......This involves giving them words of caution and warning to enable them to avoid the pitfalls they may not foresee as well as you do. It may mean providing correction.

6. *ASSETS*......This involves giving them tangible resources, gifts and tools — whether it's a book, a CD, an electronic resource or a personal contact that you can introduce to them.

7. *APPLICATION*......This involves helping them find places to apply the lessons they've learned; it means pointing out a good "laboratory" where they can practice.

All of these are gifts, given from the heart and life experience of the mentor. They become especially valuable based on the timing in which they are given. I would suggest that you look for those teachable moments, just like parents do with their children, and concentrate on giving these gifts away in those moments. My recommendation is that you memorize this list of "gifts," then be ready to give them away at any time.

Think about it. As you look over the list of gifts again, none of them have to do with possessing an extremely high IQ, lots of talent or being good looking and famous. They are gifts that anyone can give away! As mentors, we will obviously improve with time and experience, but we can all start giving these wonderful gifts to hungry mentees now. The world awaits the treasure you have to offer!

Sociologists tell us that the most introverted of persons will influence an average of 10,000 other people during his lifetime. That is a remarkable statistic to me.

If introverted, withdrawn, non-leadership-type individuals influence that many other people, imagine what kind of influence you and I who aspire to leadership might exercise! Influence is what leadership is all about. Remember, it's the simplest one-word definition of leadership. In this chapter, we will discuss how we can effectively influence a mentee through the development of specific character qualities inside us.

we must be committed

At the onset, we must make a decision to be committed people-committed to become true mentors. Several years ago I made a specific determination that I was going to mentor willing individuals for the rest of my life. That is who I have become. Commitment is what boosts us over the edge.

Perhaps you've heard of our Habitudes®. Habitudes® are "Images That Form Leadership Habits and Attitudes." One of the images in the first book of the series is called: The Half Hearted Kamikaze. It's based on a humorous illustration about a kamikaze pilot who was still alive after flying fifty missions! Something was wrong with this picture! A reporter interviewed him after his discharge from the military and asked, "How can you call yourself a kamikaze pilot, yet still be alive after so many flights?"

"Well, it's like this," the pilot responded with a grin, "I had a whole lot of involvement. Not much commitment — but a whole lot of involvement."

I believe that sounds like our generation. We sample a variety of jobs, projects, positions and activities, but often fail to be committed to one that counts. We possess a "tourist" mindset when it comes to our life.

As we consider the commitment of a mentor, we must reckon that this big commitment must be viewed from three angles:

1. *WE MUST BE COMMITTED TO A PERSON*
   Our mentees must sense our commitment to them as people. Not projects. Not duties! We must love them and have their best interests in mind. We are committed to them as an individual — not just to a large group. It is wise stewardship of our time. We must be loyal.

2. *WE MUST BE COMMITTED TO A PROCESS*
   There will be ups and downs through the season we meet with our mentees. We must step back and see the process they are in and the action steps required. We must understand the big picture of their lives. Our brains must think in processes. We must be discerning.

3. *WE MUST BE COMMITTED TO A PURPOSE*
   Our final commitment must be to the end result. We must determine that we will see them from Point "A" to Point "B" or the growth goal that you've mutually set. We must see the finished product inside our mentees and fulfill our commitment to them. Usually the mentor sees the mentee's potential sooner than they do. We must be diligent.

We should not blindly move forward into mentoring without first settling these issues. They represent fundamental commitments that provide a foundation for a healthy relationship. I suggest you carefully pray through each one of them prior to a mentorship.

developing the right qualities

I suppose the list of character qualities that mentors ought to possess could be endless. Further, if I were to simply list every ingredient that goes into the recipe for a great mentor, it would be overwhelming. That would not help us here. However, the following six words provide a guideline that is, indeed, helpful. These six terms represent major categories for you to pursue as strengths in your life as a leader and mentor. Study and memorize these words that all begin with the letter "I" and make this your "I WILL DO IT" list!

Qualities of a Good Mentor:

1. *INITIATIVE*
   - I provide direction to my relationship with my mentee and sphere of influence.
   - I take responsibility for the health of the relationship.
   - I initiate spiritual dialogue with vulnerability and humility.

2. *INTIMACY*
   - I experience healthy intimacy with my family or roommates with whom I live.
   - I experience intimacy with my mentee through open and honest conversation.

3. *INFLUENCE*
   - I exercise healthy influence in my relationship with my mentee.
   - I develop, encourage and facilitate growth in my mentee.
   - I am a "giver," a generous contributor in relationships.

4. *INTEGRITY*
   - I lead a life of integrity and honesty that is above reproach.
   - I am not ashamed of my "private" world, of who I am when no one is looking.

5. *IDENTITY*
   - I am secure in who I am; I am OK with how my personality is wired.
   - I have a healthy self-image that prevents a defensive attitude.
   - I have developed a mature statement of purpose for my life.

6. *INNER CHARACTER*
   - I exhibit self-discipline; I base my life on principals not emotions.
   - I am considered a person of strong character and one who models integrity.
   - I do not allow my gifts to carry me further than my character can sustain me.

commandments and components

In the remaining pages of this chapter I'd like to share with you what I have gleaned from men far wiser than I am. John C. Crosby and Dr. Bobby Clinton have both formed checklists of components that make a good mentoring experience. Each provides a sort of "do's and don'ts" advisory that I think is worth including here. Let's begin with Crosby's shorter list.

> **The Ten Commandments Of Mentoring**
>
> 1. *Thou shalt not play God.*
>
> 2. *Thou shalt not play Teacher.*
>
> 3. *Thou shalt not play Mother or Father.*
>
> 4. *Thou shalt not lie with your body.*
>
> 5. *Active listening is the holy time and thou shalt practice it at every session.*
>
> 6. *Thou shalt be nonjudgmental.*
>
> 7. *Thou shalt not lose heart because of repeated disappointments.*
>
> 8. *Thou shalt practice empathy, not sympathy.*
>
> 9. *Thou shalt not believe that thou can move mountains.*
>
> 10. *Thou shalt not envy thy neighbor's protégé nor thy neighbor's success.*
>
> **John C. Crosby —**
> **The Uncommon Individual Foundation**

some practical suggestions

I trust you are convinced that our world needs mentors – good mentors who want to successfully make deposits in the lives of their mentees. Let's close this chapter by getting very practical. The following "to do" lists are functions you can perform right now to become a more effective mentor.

IF YOU ARE A TEACHER...you have probably given some good thought to the subject of mentoring. But don't mistake the two. Teaching (in North America, anyway) expects the student to remain relatively passive in the learning process. We've embraced the Greek model of education which is academic and informational. The Hebrew model is based much more on relationship and experience and is transformational. Mentoring, as we have discussed already, demands relationship, conversation and some degree of shared experience. Teachers can, however, become great mentors.

Here are some suggestions about becoming a teacher who mentors effectively. These were modified from a list by Bobby Clinton:

- Catalog the major subjects you can teach so you are ready to share.
- Recognize how you would tailor them to work with an individual.
- Make it known that you have resources available to help others in the areas of your knowledge.
- Be sure to model or demonstrate the principles you are sharing.
- As you teach to impart knowledge, illustrate also the dynamics of the teaching/learning process. This motivates learners and suggests to them how and why they, too, can use the knowledge with others.
- Revise the knowledge base to fit your mentee's situation. Do not overkill. Teach what is needed.
- Challenge your mentee to use it. You do this best by demonstrating its usefulness in your own life and by showing relevancy to the mentee's situation.
- If you teach in a group context, be on the lookout for those who should be mentored individually. You can invite those who respond well into a special relationship that will allow them to move more rapidly.
- Be open to unique teaching sessions where needed. When requests come for teaching that do not fit your normal patterns, think of the possibility of empowerment for the individuals concerned. That is, be open to mentoring via teaching.

Teachers who are open to deliberate mentoring and establishing personal relationships with people in order to empower them through teaching are greatly needed. I am challenging you toward this important kind of mentoring.

IF YOU ARE A COUNSELOR...you are very often already assuming the role of a mentor with your clients. After all, therapy is speaking into the life of the counselee. The difference, however, lies in the fact that counseling is often reactive instead of proactive. It is responding to an unhealthy emotional state in someone, and therapy ends when balance comes again. Mentoring, however, should not come to closure (ideally) until the mentee is actively pursuing their role as a contributor to their world-seeking someone that they might mentor.

Since both a counselor and a mentor are guides for others, this is a good, definitive word to embrace as a role. Most people need personal guidance on emotional and spiritual issues throughout their lifetime. As a counselor, you can become an effective mentor/ guide if you'll consistently perform these functions:

- Help people assess their own development
- Point out areas of strength and weakness in their life.
- Help mentees identify needs and take initiative for change and growth.
- Provide perspectives on how to develop growth and depth.
- Provide accountability for their personal maturity.

IF YOU SIMPLY WANT TO IMPROVE YOUR MENTORING SKILLS...then I would suggest you consistently do the following list. As you do, you will increase your impact and deepen your leadership in the life of the mentee.

1. *Invest time and energy in this.* Spend some time discussing this concept of mentoring with your mentee. Have them share their perceptions of their strengths, weaknesses and openness to this process.

2. *Know yourself.* If you're going to help others in their growth, you must know your own strengths, weaknesses and personality traits. Good mentors always do.

3. *Cultivate generosity.* Good mentors have learned to be givers in relationships and realize that it is more blessed (and natural) to give then receive.

4. *Study leadership.* Read books and talk with people who can teach you how to be a better leader. You need to understand leadership issues. Good mentors always have mentors.

5. *Initiate vulnerability.* If you want an open, transparent, teachable mentee, start practicing those qualities yourself. This accelerates the growth process.

6. *Model character.* If you want to pass on a trait or skill, remember: First you do it, then you do it as the mentee observes; then he does it as you observe; then he does it – whether you're there or not.

7. *Clarify your vision.* Work to see the potential in your mentee. This will help you really believe in them. Ask Him to build in you the following qualities of a good mentor:

- Patience with people (Long-suffering)
- Ability to see the big picture (Vision)
- Commitment to relationships (Accountability)
- Enjoyment in giving (Generosity)
- Strong personal discipline (Character)
- Good communication (Communicative)
- Understanding of others (Discernment)

someone out there needs you!

I believe there is a potential "giant" somewhere out there who needs you to become their mentor. Despite your feelings of inadequacy, you need to take a step and go after them. A journey of a thousand miles begins with a single step. Sure, you will run into conflict and hardship; you may likely find a young mentee who says he or she wants to be challenged; then promptly runs from it! Go after them. Whether they know it or not, they need you.

Let me close with this analogy: Driving along a freeway one night, a woman noticed the headlights of a huge semi-truck tailgating her much too closely. She sped up, but so did the truck. She became afraid and drove even faster. Finally she exited the freeway and raced toward a nearby gas station. The truck followed her in. She leaped from her car and ran into the garage as onlookers stood by. The truck driver then climbed down from his cab, walked to her car and pulled a would-be rapist from her back seat! The trucker had spotted the man from his higher vantage point and had determined to save the woman from harm. The woman, in essence, was running from the wrong man.

In a similar way, a mentee may run from or resist the help of a mentor because of different vantage points and a misunderstanding of motives. And too often we give up our attempts to mentor because helping them is just too much of a hassle.

Trust me – there is a hassle to the business of mentoring. There are risks as well. That's why so few do it. But remember: To get to the fruit, you've got to go out on a limb.

Some years ago, our organization, Growing Leaders, created a very sticky tool for young people to learn timeless life and leadership principles. Habitudes® are images that form leadership habits and attitudes. We teach these principles through the power of a picture (check out chapter 20 to see how they work). One of my favorite Habitudes® is called: "Rivers and Floods." Think for a moment about a river and a flood. Both are bodies of water — but that's where the comparison ends. Beyond that It Is all contrast. Floods are water going in every direction. They are indiscriminate, shallow and frequently damaging. Rivers, on the other hand, are flowing in one direction because they have banks. Further, they can be very helpful if you use them correctly. You can float down a river and use it for transportation; you can light up a city with the power generated from a flowing river.

Rivers and floods remind me of the power of focus and vision. Most people are floods not rivers. They may begin well, with a single, clear vision for where they are going. But over time, especially if they've been successful, they face new options and opportunities, and what was once a river flowing in one direction becomes a flood flowing out in many directions. Most people are flooding not flowing. They are trying to "do it all," and consequently, they become five miles wide and one inch deep.

Mentors must be focused. In fact, the single greatest gift a mentor can give to a mentee is probably clear focus. That mentee likely needs clarity more than they need certainty.

Mentees should assume their role in the life of the mentee with clear focus —knowing they must provide focus to their mentee. Mentors must help mentees become rivers not floods.

Often, people fail to mentor others effectively because they are fuzzy about what the act of mentoring is supposed to accomplish. Soon, the relationship diminishes to a meeting where two people hang out and talk about sports or friends. In this chapter, let's zero in on what a mentor's focus should be and what expectations they should fulfill.

the tasks of a mentor

The following are five primary tasks that mentor should fulfill as they invest in young mentees. These tasks are central to making the relationship relevant and valuable. If a mentor does their job well, the student should be able to...

1. **DISCOVER THEIR STRENGTHS**
   I briefly mentioned this earlier. One primary task of a mentor is to enable the mentee to discover where they are strong, then remain focused on those strengths. A person's strength area will be the area where they'll have the greatest growth potential. If a mentor can help a mentee understand their strengths and begin to build a career around those strength areas, their relationship will be worth its weight in gold. A strength is simply the combination of a person's gifts and talents, their acquired skills and their knowledge.

   Far too often, we have felt it was the job of the mentor to fix the weaknesses of a mentee. While I do believe we need to remedy a mentee's character weaknesses, we should not spend the majority of our time fixing their weaknesses in talent. A person who is weak in some area will rarely get above average in that area. Why work so hard to achieve "average"? I suggest you spend that time polishing a strength area — and making someone who is good at something — excellent. People pay for excellence.

   What are some ways you can help them do this?

2. **DEVELOP THEIR CHARACTER**
   The second area to focus on is the building of the mentee's character. People generally do not develop strong character without some training and exposure.

This means you probably won't learn it from a book. You must have someone instruct you and hold you accountable; then you must watch them live it out. Character is more caught than taught. Psychologists have recently concluded that humans, indeed, have moral intelligence. What does this mean? It simply means that we have the capacity for strong character: to be honest, disciplined, ethical and secure. Here is how it works. In the same way that humans are lingual, we are moral. We all are born as lingual, meaning we have the capacity to speak a language — but we must be exposed to it before we can communicate with it. So, too, we are born with the potential to be highly moral, but we must be exposed to it before we can incarnate it.

What are some ways you can help them do this?

3. DETERMINE THEIR FOCUS
Third, a mentor must help their mentee determine their focus. Most mentees seek a mentor to determine this very thing. They feel scattered and are not sure which direction to turn. They are fuzzy not focused. Focus is a rare commodity. Once mentors work to discern the mentees strengths, it is easier to help them see what their focus should be. By "focus," I simply mean to single out the area of concentration — in their career, their studies, their investment of time, talent and money. It means helping them to locate where they should put most of their attention. This doesn't mean the gifted mentee will do less by focusing their life. It simply means they will go deeper instead of wider. Remember: What you focus on expands. When someone gains a clear focus, they begin to see layers of innovation and creativity in that area that they would not have seen going wider and skimming the surface. As a mentor, help your mentee intensify not diversify.

What are some ways you can help them do this?

4. DISCERN THEIR BLIND SPOTS
Every one of us has blind spots. Blind spots are areas of our life that we just can't or don't see clearly. Our self-awareness is low, and we need someone to help us see our state and remedy any problems that could sabotage our leadership. At some point, we are all like the female executive who returned to her table at the restaurant, unaware that she had toilet paper stuck to her stockings.

One of her colleagues gave a hand signal, but alas, she didn't get it. The toilet paper was there for all to see —except for the one it attached to it. Finally, the woman's friend asked if she could speak to her in private for just a minute. The two walked over to the restroom again to remove the appendage and be done with it. Needless to say, the woman was deeply grateful for the help. Hmmm. This is a picture of life for each of us. We need someone to help us see what we don't see, especially if it can hurt us or embarrass us.

What are some ways you can help them do this?

5. CLOSE THE GAP BETWEEN POTENTIAL AND PERFORMANCE

Finally, a mentor's job can be summarized best in this one sentence: We are to close the gap between all that potential inside our mentee and their performance. What is inside of them should come out and find expression. Talent should become performance which should become productivity. Results are the name of the game. This outcome is the product of achieving the first four of these tasks well: discovering their strengths, building strong character and preventing any character flaws, helping them to identify their focus, and opening their eyes to any blind spots they possess.

Sir Humphry Davy was a distinguished chemist during the 19th century. When he was asked late in his life what he considered to be his greatest discovery, he replied: "Michael Faraday." And, indeed, Davy was the one who found young Michael Faraday.

Davy had discovered Michael Faraday, the ignorant son of a blacksmith, taking notes at his lectures and longing to study science seriously. As Davy began to teach him, he found a brilliant mind that promised to eclipse even his own achievements. He knew that no one discovery of his own could possibly compare with the many discoveries Faraday would make during his career. Hence, his investment became a personal one into a "life" not a laboratory. You might say Davy was committed to closing the gap between Faraday's potential and his performance. In the end, both of them did a great job. Faraday changed the course of history in the field of chemistry, and Davy had the rewarding experience of helping him reach his potential.

What are some ways you can help them do this?

let's go to the movies...

Over the years, Hollywood has produced a number of films that move audiences emotionally because they provide stories of mentors and mentees. These stories reveal how one person practiced the five roles above — helping someone else find their strength, build their character, choose their focus, see their blind spots and reach their potential. Even when the word "mentor" is not used in these films, we still feel the emotion of it because the story contains some developmental relationship where one person empowers another person along the way. Some examples have been...

- *Stand and Deliver*
- *Dead Poet's Society*
- *Karate Kid*
- *Finding Forrester*
- *Lead the Way*
- *Freedom Writers*
- *Mr. Holland's Opus*

Reflect on these films for a moment. What are the similarities they share? What one thing do they all have in common? What are some current examples of films or programs containing a life-changing mentor? What common threads do you see in them?

The stories will all be different, involving different people, genders, ages, challenges and outcomes. But they will all be about someone adding value to another by helping them become clear on their direction. That's it. Mentors bring clarity on the direction of someone else's life.

the good news

The good news is mentors do not have to share identical experiences with their mentee in order to help them. In other words, it is not required that mentors possess expertise and experience in the areas they are coaching their mentee. It helps, but it is not necessary. They simply must be able to see what the mentee cannot see, provide some clarification, support them and hold them accountable until they make progress. My friend Andy Stanley told me recently that he's coached a number of mentees in areas he is not an expert. That may shock you, but here is what he told me. He was simply able to see something they were not and understood the steps they could take to get them to their goal.

Let me summarize:

Notify
Mentors must see what the mentee cannot and share it with him or her.

Clarify
Mentors must provide some clarification on the focus for the mentee.

Demystify
Mentors must offer direction; clear action steps to the mentee.

Fortify
Mentors must support and encourage the mentee to take those steps.

Intensify
Mentors must hold the mentee accountable until progress is made.

That's it. Mentoring doesn't have to be complex. It is about doing these simple tasks for someone you believe in. It is labor, but in many ways, it is simply unleashing a mentee to labor in the areas they should be focusing on anyway. The mentee is the player. The mentor is the coach.

One morning, a third grade boy asked his teacher if she got paid for teaching. When she smiled and said, "Yes," he responded, "That's funny. We do all the work."

It may feel this way to your mentee at times, but when you perform these tasks you are providing a gift that is priceless.

It was a Romanian bishop who first spoke these profound words to me: "Success... without a successor... is a failure."

Read that again. That one phrase captures the heartbeat of mentoring. Each of us who mentor wants to do it well. We want to see our mentees take what we've given them and flourish with it. They are, in many ways, the next generation the "successors" that will follow us in life. If we didn't believe in building successors, we probably wouldn't be mentoring. This chapter concerns itself with enabling you to mentor well. I hope to put some fundamental tools in your toolbox that will help you do it successfully.

Bobb Biehl, head of Masterplanning Group International, shares these paraphrased thoughts about the core of successful mentoring.

When people hear the word mentor, they tend to think of a white-haired person who is old and feeble and/or rich and famous. And when they hear the word protégé, they tend to think of a kid on a piano bench learning the keyboard from the maestro.

But in reality, the mentor-protégé relationship in its simplest form is a lot like a big brother, big sister relationship. The big brother really wants to see the little brother win. It isn't that the mentor has to be older. But he or she must want very badly to see another person win and be committed to helping them win.

One of my favorite portraits of a mentor went on display before the entire world at the 1992 Summer Olympics in Barcelona, Spain. Derrick Redman, an athlete from England, had qualified to compete in the 440 meter event despite the fact that he'd had 22 surgeries on his Achilles heel. It was a miracle to some that he was even able to run again, not to mention qualify for the Olympics.

It was at the event, however, that tragedy struck. Midway through the race Derrick Redman pulled up short and fell to the ground. He had pulled a hamstring and faced still another injury. At least one of the cameras stayed glued to this athlete as he got up and limped forward, wincing in pain. He could barely stay on his feet. His hopes of winning were dashed, and while he wanted desperately to finish the race, even this looked impossible. Derrick wept as he realized it was all over for him.

Enter his mentor. Sitting in the stands, second row from the top, was Jim Redman, Derrick's father and mentor. He could not imagine doing anything else but getting involved. He pushed his way past the huge crowd separating him from the track. He persistently moved toward the gate and sifted through the security guards. They would not keep this man from his mentee. Jim had been Derrick's biggest fan through the years, and this move was the only logical one for him. The cameras quickly focused on this intruder running toward the pitiful athlete from the UK. Jim put his arm around his son, and it must have been a familiar touch because Derrick took a few more steps and stopped. In tears, Derrick fell into his lather's arms and wept. The two exchanged words for a moment. I am sure Jim asked Derrick if he was sure he wanted to finish the race. When Derrick replied that he did, Jim said what I consider to be classic mentor words: "Derrick, we started this thing together. We are going to finish this thing together." Then Jim did what all great mentors do for their mentees. Jim lifted Derrick up, put his son's arm over his own shoulder, and the two finished the 400 meter race together.

I remember watching this scene with tears in my eyes. I had not expected to observe such an act of love that day — to receive such a clear snapshot of someone investing in the life of another. I can remember the crowd applauding for the two of them as they finished the race arm in arm, as loudly as they did the winner of the race that day. Whether he knew it or not, Jim Redman gave the world a picture of a mentor: One who picks up the life of another and says, "I'm going to help you finish your race well."

the different kinds of mentors

This is something every one of us can do for someone else. If you are not mentoring now, it may be because you don't feel you have what it takes to be a mentor. Like so many others, you may feel you have neither the time nor the talent to give. If so, let me liberate you. You actually can mentor others well, but you may have to change your mental image of a mentor.

Knowing your personal style and gifts will enable you to better decide what kind of mentor you need (for yourself) at this season in your life and what role you will best fulfill in a mentee's life. Often, we possess stereotypes about what a true "mentor" looks like. As I mentioned, we often picture some wise, old guru who has nuggets of wisdom spilling out in every conversation. This prevents some potential mentors from starting. We're afraid we won't measure up. I believe we must scrap those stereotypes.

Years ago, Bobby Clinton and Paul Stanley wrote about different kinds of mentors in their book called Connecting. They suggest there may not be one, single type of mentor that suits everyone. I concur. In fact, inspired by their writings, I have created a list of the different kinds of mentors below. This list will benefit you in two ways:

1. It will reveal to you what you are best suited to become for a mentee.

2. It will reveal what you need yourself at different stages of your life.

Different Kinds of Mentors:

DIRECTOR
This mentor provides personal/career direction, accountability, insight for maturation.

CONSULTANT
This mentor is on-call as important decisions are made; meeting at forks in the road.

COACH
The mentor who offers motivation and skills needed to meet a task or a challenge.

TEACHER
The mentor who gives wisdom, understanding and knowledge on a given subject.

COUNSELOR
This mentor furnishes big picture perspective; they give a 35,000 foot fly over to life.

SPONSOR
The mentor connects a mentee with resources: a personal network, a book, an article.

MODEL
The mentor who exemplifies a model life or career; they incarnate the principles in their lifestyle.

You will observe that each of these roles provides a different kind of service to someone. Some are best suited for close, regular inspections of the personal life of the mentee. The director, for example, is needed most in a mentee's early career days. Frequency of meetings and strict enforcement of accountability are more essential during those days than for a less mature, inexperienced mentee. Later in their lives, they may not need the same kind of questions to be asked by their mentor. In fact, the mentor they need at that point is very different. As a mature person, they need more consultant-type meetings which could be less frequent, but the issues are deeper. The bottom line is: We need different kinds of mentors at different stages of life.

This list of various mentor roles can be liberating. First, because it prevents us from an unrealistic pursuit of one ideal mentor or a pursuit to become an ideal, perfect mentor. Second, it can help all of us see which role we are best suited to play. I, for one, am much better suited to meet with mature mentees who may be preparing for leadership than with younger students exploring the details of their college major. I have done both, and I am more fulfilled at playing the former role; it fits my style and gifts far better. Third, the list of seven roles serves as a guide for us in the different seasons of our lives. Right now I do not need a director as much as I need a coach and a sponsor. All of this should spark us to seek these key relationships. I mention more than once in this book that I have six mentors in my life right now. Each year, I choose a handful of people to meet with who have strengths in areas in which I want to grow. I do not expect one person to have all the answers to all my questions. Each one is a mentor in a specialized area.

can he? will he?

A lot of men and women are successful managers. They've effectively managed their own company, military platoon, school, church or other type of organization. They have built a team of people into a well-oiled machine. It's that sound management that brings the feeling of success. Eventually, however, deep down inside they begin to think: I wonder who I could develop and bring along as a protégé. They know that true success means building something that outlasts their own lives. It means they must do more than be efficient — they must be effective.

Mal King, in the manuscript for his book, *Mentoring: The Only Way To Develop Leaders*, paraphrases Ashley Montagu's definition of love as it applies to mentoring:

> "Mentoring is the demonstrated, active involvement in the welfare of another in such a way that one not only contributes to the survival of the other, but does so in a creatively enlarging manner, in a manner calculated to stimulate the potentialities of the other so that they may develop to their optimum capacity. It is to communicate to the other that one is profoundly interested in him, that one is there to offer him all the supports and stimulations he requires for the realization of his potentialities for being a person able to relate himself to others in a creatively enlarging manner, who gives the psychological support and sustenance the other requires, to nourish and to enable him to grow not only in his potentialities for being a human being but also to train him in the development of those inner controls that will make external ones unnecessary."

Wow! What a snapshot of a mentor. Clearly, Bobb Biehl and Mal King give us at least a blueprint from which to operate. Our work is cut out for us. But before we itemize the details of what makes a successful mentor, let's briefly examine the pitfalls we must avoid. In the same way that we all hold incredible potential for developing people successfully, we all hold the opportunity to damage them as well. Authority can be abused; ignorance can prevent us from doing what we ought; lack of discernment may cause us to say something hurtful or mistaken.

The following list was first developed by Richard H. Tyre for The Uncommon Individual Foundation. He calls it:

how to spot a toxic mentor

1. The Avoider
"Of course we 'll get together, but I'm too busy today."
Initial enthusiasm but later inaccessibility. Not available when the need is greatest. Cannot get close emotionally. Unintentionally forgets to share organizational information or helpful personal affirmation.

2. The Dumper
"A protégé? I'd love a dedicated assistant!"
Opposite to the Avoider. Is delighted to give the mentee opportunities, assignments, extra work, more responsibility, but gives inadequate guidance; the mentee is abandoned. All that is given is work.

3. The Criticizer
"Let me take this opportunity to show you why that's not the right way to do it."
Believes mentoring is a license to point out mistakes. Gives the mentee responsibility – maybe too much, too soon – and then criticizes them for inexperience and poor performance. Unconsciously keeps them subordinate.

4. The User
"My wife doesn't understand me. You're not breaking up anything; we're already distant."
The mentee is the mentor's spy in the ranks. They run up the flags. They are a convenient, pleasant companion, backboard or source of ideas. They are used for the mentor's benefit, not necessarily the mentee's.

5. The Black Halo
"They don't know what they're doing. Let me show you how to do it."
You have the perfect mentor. Unfortunately, anyone associated with this person becomes poison in the organization. The mentor teaches the mentee all there is to know, but policy has changed, and his way of operating is out of favor.

6. The Queen Bee
"I made it in a much tougher time by myself. You can, too."
This mentor doesn't believe the mentee should show a need for help. They believe the Attrition Theory: "I made it by hard work, brains and luck, but they made it by knowing someone!" The mentee feels inferior.

what is a successful mentor, anyway?
In our context a successful mentor is one who assumes responsibility for the development of his mentee. The key term is "development." The successful mentor is going to be a:

• Guide
• Encourager
• Resource
• Evaluator
• Provider

When I think of the term "mentor," it conjures up images I have mentioned earlier: images of a tradesman or craftsman developing a young apprentice in old England. Can you see it? Cobblestone streets with horses and carriages, a shop off the main street where this craftsman works — all the while being observed by an up-and-coming young man who one day wants to own a shop of his own. The craftsman spends time explaining his work to the curious, onlooking apprentice, allowing him to try his hand at doing the work himself to gain the skill, then debriefing the young man at the close of the day. What a beautiful analogy for the mentor today.

Dr. Tony Campolo, in his book, *Who Switched the Price Tags?*, reports the results of a survey of retired people living in their twilight years. In response to the question, "If you could live your life over again, what changes would you make?" they shared three common answers:

• I would reflect more. *(I would take the time to stop and make sense of my journey.)*
• I would risk more. *(I played it too safe. I would take more risks in the areas that count.)*
• I would invest my life in areas that will outlive me. *(I would try to leave a legacy by investing in the lives of others.)*

All three answers are insightful, but read the third one again. That statement is the vision and fruit of a mentor. It is pouring your life, wisdom, skills and spirit into the life of another so that there is leadership reproduction — life multiplication. Does this sound strangely familiar? It is just like parenting. It is giving birth to someone like yourself, then providing the tools for them to succeed in life and reproduce themselves in the life of a third generation. Might that best begin with those already in our sphere of influence? Mentoring is the ultimate acid-test of leadership.

I cannot think of a wiser investment of our time and energy than in the people who are right under our noses. They are immortal souls with potential and gifts within them. I believe we were designed for that kind of fulfilling, satisfying investment – an investment that lasts. A television interview reminded me of this some years ago. Just after the annual Rose Bowl Parade in Pasadena, California, a young float builder was interviewed and asked whether he enjoyed constructing those huge, multifaceted floats each year. When he replied that he did, he was asked if he had considered doing it as a career. His response was a decisive "No," and then he explained why: "I could never imagine investing so much of myself into something that's thrown into the scrap pile within a matter of weeks." Great insight! How often do we sell ourselves short by investing so much in insignificant, temporal and trivial causes? We give so much time to things that don't really matter.

About a hundred years ago, a young boy was scarred for life by his parents as he grew up during World War I in Germany. His family, the Schicklewubers, had developed distorted priorities that left the boy emotionally alone and confused. He overheard his father talk about moving away one evening, and assumed that he would be abandoned. He decided then to toughen up and find refuge in things outside of love and family. He would never let someone inside his heart again. The world has suffered much from that decision; for you and I know this young boy as Nazi dictator Adolf Hitler. I have to wonder how history might have been altered if young Adolf had had a wise mentor available to him.

This chapter deals with the least popular element of mentoring: confrontation. No healthy, balanced person actually enjoys the act of confronting someone over a bad attitude, a flaw, gossip, insubordination or failure to follow-through on a commitment. Those kinds of meetings always seem to cause our stomachs to churn, our hands and heads to sweat, and our wills to weaken. We can and should learn to love the fruit of such interaction, but only a sadistic person enjoys the act of confrontation!

Even the word "confront" is a heavy word. It seems so demeaning, so warlike. I believe we ought to make an adjustment right off the bat if we're going to engage in confrontation effectively. Dr. John Maxwell suggests that we should use the word "clarification" more often than "confrontation." It paints a more relational picture. Most of the time, when there is a problem, we are merely clarifying a misunderstanding or miscommunication anyway. When we approach our mentee with the attitude that we simply want to clarify rather than indict them or punish them for their obvious failure. We are able to maintain a much more loving and compassionate demeanor. Good advice.

laying foundation

When our mentees have done an apparent wrong, and we believe it is significant enough to discuss it with them, we need to operate from a moral foundation. If you are wavering over whether it is right to confront, always check your motives. Ask yourself: "Why do I believe I need to confront them? What is my goal? Is it for their benefit or for my relief?"

101

In addition, keep the following statements in mind, as you consider the discussion with your mentee. The statements represent the right motivation for confrontation. They contain the objectives you'll want to embrace in your meeting. These are why you must confront when appropriate.

- You want to see them transformed into a healthy, effective leader.
- The goal is not condemnation, but restoration.
- Challenging them to grow must go beyond good advice.
- People need help with the practical application of truth.
- We must love truth more than anything else in this world.
- Most people know the truth but believe a lie about their own reality.

Kent Amos, former Xerox executive and later head of the Washington based Urban Family Institute, said recently: "We never think of helping troubled young people to change their lives by giving them the guidance and education and training they need. Instead, we think punitively: Three strikes, and you're out. Two years, and you're off welfare — even if you have no place else to go."

In many ways, he's right. It's time we become proactive with our attention toward this generation. It's time we "build a fence at the top of the cliff rather than a hospital at the bottom." The only way we can succeed in this preventative way is to confront issues before it's too late.

steps toward effective confrontation

I've lost count of the number of occasions where I had to confront a person who I was mentoring. I would often try to talk myself out of doing it, thinking that if I just ignored the problem it would go away. That, of course, is rarely true. I have never regretted confronting a situation when I did it in a healthy way. In fact, at this point in my life I believe successful confrontation was the most important lesson I learned as young leader. The following list represents the steps I generally take when confronting a mentee. Keep in mind that confrontation (or clarification) is right only when the issue is clear (i.e., the mentee is damaging themselves, someone else or failing to keep a commitment you've agreed upon). When this is the case,

I recommend this process:

1. **WORK THROUGH YOUR ANGER**
   Don't let emotion lead you. Wait until you're objective, but try to deal with issues before they become big ones. Don't let issues get bottled up inside of you.

2. **INITIATE THE CONTACT**
   Don't wait for them to initiate. Mentors and leaders must be proactive to make things right whether you're the offender or the offended.

3. **BEGIN WITH AFFIRMATION**
   Speak words of belief and encouragement first. Then receive fresh permission to challenge them.

4. **TELL THEM YOU HAVE A PROBLEM OR STRUGGLE**
   Don't hint that it's their problem, but yours; own the fact that you are wrestling with an issue.

5. **BRING UP THE ISSUE. AND EXPLAIN YOU DON'T UNDERSTAND**
   Aim to clarify. Ask questions. Always give them the benefit of the doubt. Believe the best and allow them to explain themselves. When you speak, however, be clear and firm.

6. **LISTEN AND ALLOW THEM TO RESPOND**
   At this point, it's your turn to listen. Allow them to respond to the issue. Commit yourself to actively engage in listening.

7. **ESTABLISH FORGIVENESS AND REPENTANCE**
   See them at their best. Be redemptive as you talk. Seek restoration of the relationship. Don't conclude until forgiveness is extended and issues resolved.

8. **COMPROMISE ON OPINIONS, NOT ON PRINCIPLES**
   Determine what you'll die for. Be flexible with your opinions, but not with your values or principles. Be gracious when you can; be firm when you must.

9. **COME UP WITH A PLAN**
   Together, attempt to work on action steps to remedy the issue. Be sure you both have "skin in the game." Sacrifice to make things work.

10. AFFIRM YOUR PURPOSE AND YOUR LOVE AS YOU CONCLUDE
Always close these times on a positive note if possible. Give them hope with your words.

An unexamined life, said Socrates, is not worth living. A mentor's wounds are those of a faithful friend. Not everyone has the right to climb into a mentee's life and offer rebuke. It must be the mentor who has built a trusting relationship beforehand. Alfred Whitehead once said, "Apart from blunt truth, our lives sink decadently amid the perfume of hints and suggestions." At the same time, we must earn our right to speak such words. For years, I have tried to live by this axiom: We must build bridges of relationship that can bear the weight of truth.

Chuck Swindoll tells the story of a lady who made an appointment with a pastor to talk about joining his church. She said the surgeon who had performed her face-lift told her, "My dear, I have done an extraordinary job on your face, as you can see in the mirror. I have charged you a great deal of money and you were happy to pay it. But I want to give you some free advice. Find a group of people who love God and who will love you enough to help you deal with all of the negative emotions inside of you. If you don't, you'll be back in my office in a short time with your face in far worse shape than before."

your attitude
Very likely, the attitude you have when you are confronting/clarifying will be more important than the words you speak. Do your best to embrace these additional principles when meeting with your mentee:

- *BE GENEROUS (Both words and actions)*
- *BELIEVE IN PEOPLE*
- *STAY LOYAL*
- *TAKE A STAND*
- *GET EXCITED ABOUT ANY IMPROVEMENT*
- *AFFIRM PEOPLE*

Affirming your belief in your mentee is never more crucial than when you are confronting/clarifying a tough issue in their life. They must know, beyond a shadow of a doubt, you believe in them. Dale Carnegie illustrates this need with the following story:

In the early 19th century, a young man in London aspired to be a writer. But everything seemed to be against him. He had not been able to attend school more than four years. His father had been thrown in jail because he couldn't pay his debts, and this young man often knew the pangs of hunger.

Finally he got a job pasting labels on bottles in a rat-infested warehouse, and he slept at night in a dismal attic room with two other boys — guttersnipes from the slums of London. He had so little confidence in his ability to write that he sneaked out and mailed his first manuscript in the dead of the night so nobody would laugh at him. Story after story was refused. Finally the great day came when one was accepted. True, he wasn't paid for it, but one editor had praised him. One editor had given him recognition. He was so thrilled that he wandered about aimlessly around the streets with tears rolling down his cheeks.

The praise and recognition he received through getting one story in print changed his whole life. If it hadn't been for that encouragement, he might have spent his entire life working in rat infested factories. You may have heard of that boy. His name is Charles Dickens.

the application of accountability

The term "accountability" has become another popular word in the day we live. It has been defined in a number of elaborate ways. My favorite definition for it is simply to help people keep their commitments. When you hold someone accountable you are simply helping them live the life they want to love. Period. I suggest you and your mentee discuss the five toughest areas of discipline (or values) for each of you at the beginning of your relationship (these may include lust, lack of discipline, not sticking to a budget, thought life, gossip, etc.). Then exchange your lists and invite each other to ask about those areas on a regular basis. Always close the question/answer period with: "Have you been completely honest with your responses?"

Let me close this chapter by posing some personal questions of my own to you.

1. Is someone accountable to you so that you can make them accountable for their own growth?

2. Can you name one or more people outside your family to whom you've made yourself accountable?

3. Are you aware of the dangers of no accountability — dangers such as blind spots, unhealthy relationships, unspoken motives that will never be known without such a friend?

4. When was the last time you gave an account for the private areas of your life to someone outside your family? This would include your finances, occupational diligence or lack of it, your attitude at the office or packing too much work in each day.

5. Is anyone appraising your leadership?

6. How about your struggles with bad habits?

As a mentor, develop the courage and the right motive to confront. For the good of the protégé and for the good of the world they will soon impact. One word of truth outweighs the world. And one mentor who speaks the truth impacts the whole world. That mentor can be you.

Sooner or later I suppose every one of us longs to speak with authority when addressing that special "someone" in our life. Parents pray for authority as their children become teenagers and test every boundary in front of them. Coaches long for it as they encounter key players or crucial games during the season. Teachers wish they had it as they speak to troublemakers in class. Pastors consistently look for ways to gain authority and influence in the lives of the people in their congregations.

Clearly, this is one of the central issues in the life of a mentor as well. How can I speak into the life of my mentee and be relevant, profound, timely and life transforming? How can I share with them in such a way that it empowers them? How can my words carry weight so that the mentee not only listens to them but trusts them enough to act on them?

Obviously, not everything we say should carry that much weight. We are human and sometimes hold opinions that are faulty. From time to time, however, we really want to be heard — and ought to be heard — by those we invest in. As mentors, there are times (like it or not) when our words are important. Our mentees will listen to them, remember them and act on them. This is a sobering thought. It is a responsible position to be in, and it's our humbling privilege to exercise this role.

My favorite movie I saw in 1996 was a film called *Mr. Holland's Opus*. Perhaps you saw it, too. I love the movie because it tells the story of a reluctant mentor.

Glen Holland (played by Richard Dreyfuss) is a musician who possesses one goal in life: to get rich and famous by composing a symphony in New York. In order to save up enough money to get to New York, he takes a job at a local high school teaching music. He plans to teach for just three years, but along the way, the students begin to get under his skin. Although he doesn't even like them, Mr. Holland observes their needs and feels as though he should help them. Early in the film, a red-haired girl with pigtails asks if he can tutor her in the clarinet. He reluctantly agrees to meet her outside of class and soon learns that the real issue of her life is not playing the clarinet. It is her self-esteem. Her sister is so smart, and she feels so stupid. In response, Mr. Holland speaks words of affirmation and navigation; he tells her he sees potential inside of her. Later, he is confronted by another student in need, and then another and another. For most of the story, Mr. Holland is speaking into the lives of teenage students hesitantly and reluctantly. He remains at the school not for three years, but for thirty.

In the end, it all comes crashing down. Mr. Holland is called into the principal's office and given some bad news. Due to budget cuts in the district, all music classes must be cut from the curriculum. He cannot believe it. He is in stunned silence. When he stands up, he is angry; he is shaking, he threatens to appeal before the board of education. When he does, his appeal is rejected. Mr. Holland's career is over.

In one final scene, he enters his dark, empty music room one last time. When a colleague sees him, and asks if he is ok, Glen puts into words everything he is thinking. He admits he should be laughing. "It's funny," he says. "They drug me into this gig kicking and screaming, and now it's the only thing I want to do." Then, he begins to get pensive. He stares blankly at the walls and acknowledges he doesn't understand what's happened. "You work your whole life," he says, "because you think that what you do really counts. That you matter to somebody. Then, suddenly, you get a wake up call that says, 'No, you are mistaken. You are expendable.'" What is behind his groans is the fact that he could be in New York at that point with some money in his pocket. Instead, he has nothing. He has wasted his career.

When he leaves the room, he is joined by his wife and son. They walked down that long dark hallway one last time. When they reach the lobby, however, they hear a noise coming from the auditorium. It is music. He wonders what it is and walks over to the doorway to check it out.

When he opens the doors, he is blown away. The auditorium is full of students — his students — both current students and alumni, who have come to say thank you for investing his life in theirs. The crowd represents thirty years of students from 1965 to 1995. He cannot believe it. They have gathered to say farewell.

Then, the state governor stepped up to the podium. She happened to be the red-haired girl Mr. Holland had mentored in 1965. In that moment, she summarized the power of Mr. Holland's decision to work at that school. She said, "Rumor has it that Mr. Holland feels like his life is a failure because he always wanted to get to New York and get rich or famous (probably both), composing a symphony. This symphony was going to be the climax to his life." Then, she paused and looked right at him. "But Mr. Holland never made it to New York. He never got rich off of the school salaries here, and never got famous outside of this school." Another pause as she stared for a moment right at Glen Holland. Then, with a smile she concluded, "But Mr. Holland, if you feel your life is a failure that would be where you are wrong. Just look around you. We are your symphony. We are the notes of your opus."

Suddenly, Mr. Holland was in tears as he reflects on her words. She was right. He made the right decision by working with students rather than choosing the money in New York. He had the privilege of speaking into the lives of kids and would transform them without even knowing it.

"Speaking into the life" of your mentee is a learned art. Speaking with authority is an earned right. Both what you learn and earn can increase your influence with them. Let's take a look at both of these components.

speaking into their life

I love the term "speaking into their life." It implies that we are speaking personally and intimately to them. It also implies that we are speaking words of direction or perspective that will impact them. It means speaking to a relevant need in their life and empowering them with our words. It may mean speaking words of vision for their future.

The first evidence we see of this practice is in the ancient scriptures when patriarchs would bless their sons. Back then it was common for Hebrew fathers to speak words of blessing (affirmation and direction) to their children as they grew into adulthood. It was a "rite of passage" for young men.

109

We read in the book of Genesis about Jacob blessing his sons with specific words of affirmation for each of them. It was as though these fathers knew the intrinsic need we all have for someone in authority to believe in us and tell us so. Authors Gary Smalley and John Trent have written an excellent book called, The Blessing. In it they describe the five elements of this blessing that we can practice today.

The Blessing Consists Of...

1. *Meaningful Touch*

2. *Spoken Word*

3. *Expression of High Value*

4. *Description of a Special Future (Word Pictures)*

5. *Application of Genuine Commitment*

We live in an age where people seem more wounded than ever. It is now common to grow up in a world involving divorce, abuse, dysfunction, incest, neglect, addictive behavior or co-dependent relationships. Needy people are everywhere. So, how does this affect our mentoring? Do we simply try to avoid these issues? Do we ignore them or pretend they aren't there? Obviously, we can't do this if we intend to lead well. Instead, we must recover this practice performed by Hebrew leaders (patriarchs and priests) with their people and families. This practice came to be known as "giving the blessing" to others. Because most families don't practice giving this "blessing" to each other, I believe mentors must pick up the slack and do it for their mentees. It is up to us.

what's happened to us?

Allow me to be blunt. It seems the majority of people I meet today are insecure and have lost their sense of significance. Or, they cover it up. People go to great lengths to protect the image of "I've got everything under control." But it's a facade. I believe most people you'll mentor will struggle with emotional wounds from the past. Consequently, they may be unclear about their own identity. These past wounds cause gifted people to miss their potential. They cause smart people to do dumb things. They cause potentially great leaders to sabotage themselves. It's a struggle we all have to some degree. Why?

We try to solve deep needs with superficial solutions. We cover up our hurts with sarcasm or humor. We compensate for our feelings of inadequacy by becoming workaholics. These are cosmetic solutions. We get lost in the noise to cover it up. Our personal needs go unmet or are met in an unhealthy way. We don't know what to call it, but people everywhere are searching for "the blessing." We long for someone's approval; for someone to affirm that we're "OK" and that we matter and that we contribute to a cause bigger than ourselves. I believe people struggle today with a need for the blessing. Note the following four components necessary for inner health:

1. A SENSE OF WORTH. IF MISSING, WE FEEL INFERIOR.

2. A SENSE OF BELONGING. IF MISSING, WE FEEL INSECURE.

3. A SENSE OF COMPETENCE. IF MISSING, WE FEEL INADEQUATE.

4. A SENSE OF PURPOSE. IF MISSING, WE FEEL INSIGNIFICANT.

spotting the symptoms

How do we know when the blessing has not been received by our mentee? There is no scientific formula to answer that question. However, the following symptoms are often clues to the absence of the blessing:

- Hostile Spirit (Angry at the lack of approval)
- Ungrateful Spirit (Presumptive that they deserve favors)
- Insecurity (Feeling unsure about the acceptance of others)
- Inexpressive Demeanor (The withdrawal from others due to the fear of risk)
- Independent Spirit (Deciding they must fend for themselves)
- Driven Spirit (Determined to achieve and get noticed)
- Tendency to Sabotage Self (Undermining progress because they don't deserve it)
- Co-Dependency (Needing to be needed; rescuer or needs to be rescued)

People attempt to meet the need for security and significance through many artificial means. You may recognize some of the following sources we look to for our identity:
1. Performance
2. Possessions

111

3. *Pleasure*
4. *Power*
5. *People (relationships)*

As I mentioned, if a natural authority figure (i.e., parent) has neglected or been unable to give the blessing to their child, then mentors must step forward to bless them and instill the necessary confidence and competence.

Through healthy physical touch and hugs, verbal expressions of affirmation and casting clear vision for what they could become, mentees can grow far beyond their expectations and further than what a classroom could ever accomplish. Reflect for a moment on a Jewish bar mitzvah or bat mitzvah. Their significance is not that the young person being honored learns some new piece of information. It is, instead, the fact that several adults — authority figures — focus their attention and belief on that young person. These ceremonies have more to do with the heart than the head.

the root and fruit of our behavior

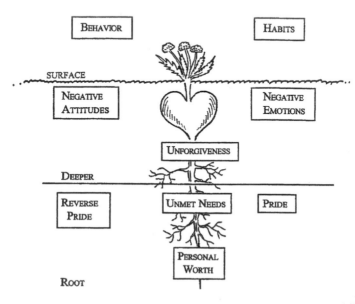

exhibit 14-1

Notice the diagram on the previous page, entitled Exhibit 14-1. I believe it illustrates what every mentor should know about their mentee. It is a graphic of a weed and its root. The weed represents the negative behavior or habits you can see. The root represents the internal conflict (below the surface) you cannot see. The point is, for every weed in our lives, there is a root cause. Usually it involves a person whom we believe has failed us. Going deeper, we often cannot forgive them because we expected them to meet a need in our life. When they cannot meet that need, we feel we cannot forgive them.

Ultimately, when you probe deeper, the real issue to resolve is self-worth. At the end of the day, our value should come from a source transcendent of human approval. As young people, we seek human approval. Eventually, we must come to the place where our worth is found in something beyond human approval. In other words, we should not place our emotional health in the hands of a person. I believe mentors must bless their mentee until they buy in to their own self-worth. Their identity is solid, based upon a set of beliefs and values they live by.

speaking with authority
Now that we've defined what it means to "speak into the life" of someone, let's examine how we can do all of this with authority. Gaining authority in someone's life doesn't come easily or naturally unless you are their parent; even then it may be difficult! To have authority means to carry influence with a mentee.

strong leadership equals deep influence

So, how do we earn deep influence in a mentee's life? Good question. The best way to answer it may be for you to think of the influential people in YOUR past. Perhaps it was a teacher or a parent, a coach or a youth pastor. Can you think of someone? Now ask yourself: "How did they gain influence in my life?" Your answer may tell you what you must do with your mentee. They likely spent quality time with you; they probably believed in you and really seemed to care about your life. I'm sure they were genuine and encouraging. Most of these ingredients that earn deep influence in a mentee have to do with ATTITUDE, not APTITUDE. They have to do with our heart more than our head and can be implemented by every one of us today. We do NOT need greater talents, higher IQ or more skills. We must simply decide to do what we know to do.

To summarize, I have taken the word "INFLUENCE" and used each letter to remind you of what good leaders have done to gain influence in the life of individuals. If you'll practice these nine elements, you'll be influential.

how to gain influence with people
Let's take a look at what these qualities mean in detail. Remember, each of these qualities have more to do with your heart and your attitude than they do with your gifts and your intelligence. Study them and reflect on how you might apply them.

I - *INVESTMENT IN PEOPLE*
Great mentors make deliberate deposits in the lives of people.

N - *NATURAL WITH PEOPLE*
Great mentors are genuine and don't try to hide their humanity.

F - *FAITH IN PEOPLE*
Great mentors are optimists and believe in their mentees.

L - *LISTENING TO PEOPLE*
Great mentors earn their right to speak through active listening.

U - *UNDERSTANDING OF PEOPLE*
Great mentors have a keen discernment about what makes people tick.

E - *ENCOURAGER TO PEOPLE*
Great mentors naturally find the good in others and affirm it.

N - *NAVIGATE FOR PEOPLE*
Great mentors offer wise words of direction and uncover the best options.

C - *CONCERN FOR PEOPLE*
Great mentors give love and compassion to others.

E - *ENTHUSIASM OVER PEOPLE*
Great mentors exhibit a zeal and passion for those they invest in.

bethany's story

When my two children turned thirteen, I determined I wanted to provide this rite-of-passage to them. My wife and I noticed it was time to introduce other voices in their lives besides our own. This is helpful when students enter their teenage years. So we made what was probably the smartest parenting decision of our lives.

When our daughter, Bethany, was thirteen, we sat down with her one night and talked about the significance of that year for her — it was a year she would begin to pass from childhood to womanhood. Then, I suggested this plan. We would choose six women in her life that we would ask to be one-day mentors for her. Women that she thought were cool and ones her mother and I respected. It didn't take us long to choose the mentors.

Next, I called each one and asked if they would invest a day in our daughter's life. I told them if they worked, they could take Bethany to work with them. In fact, they could put her to work. My only request was that they each share one "life message" with our daughter; something they wish someone had shared with them when they were thirteen.

These women were amazing. Not only did they all say "yes," but they also went beyond our wildest imaginations. Sara, an RN, took Bethany to a maternity ward in the hospital. Our daughter helped mothers give birth to babies all day long. Later that afternoon, Sara took her to a class for unwed mothers, and Bethany sat in a room full of other young teens who were pregnant. Most of them had gotten pregnant prematurely and weren't really ready for the responsibility of motherhood. It was as sobering as the maternity ward. Finally, at the end of the day, Sara's life message for Bethany was on sexual purity. Waiting for the right man before she said "yes." You can imagine this message was incredibly profound after the day they spent together — much more memorable than my lecture on the subject. Holly, another mentor, took Bethany to downtown Atlanta, where they worked in the projects all day, among homeless families. Betsy, a flight attendant with Delta airlines, surprised Bethany by flying her up to New York City for the day. Each woman had their own special message and their own unique environment to share it.

At the end of the year, we hosted a dinner and invited each mentor to our home to say thanks. Bethany served and ate with them before we migrated into the family room for a time to talk.

115

At this point, our thirteen-year-old daughter sat in the middle of the room with her mentors all around her — and one by one, she read a personal thank you card she had written, outlining the significant lesson she remembered from their time together. It was emotionally moving. Finally, I opened up the scriptures and read how Jewish families would give the blessing to their children. Before I could suggest that we repeat that same act with Bethany, those women gathered near our daughter as she sat in the midst of them, and they began to speak into her life. They spoke words of blessing, reminding her of how much they believed in her, how much they loved her and how much potential they could see in her future. There wasn't a dry eye in the room. As the evening ended, Bethany presented each of them with a gift. It was a memorable night.

I smiled as I tucked my son, Jonathan, into bed that night. Since he was the younger brother by four years, he was poised, watching the events of the evening in wonderment. As I pulled the blanket up over him to say goodnight, he looked up at me and said, "Dad, I already have the six guys chosen that I want to mentor me."

Perhaps you heard the story of the taxi cab driver and the preacher who both died and entered heaven the same day. St. Peter met them at the pearly gate and led them to their mansions. The taxi cab driver was directed to a huge, luxurious mansion; the preacher was then shown his tiny, beaten-up one-room shack. Needless to say, the cabby was elated, and the preacher was livid with anger. "I want an explanation!" screamed the clergyman. "You gave the cab driver a mansion, and although I pastored for over forty years in churches, you gave me a pitiful shack! How can you do this?" St. Peter smiled. "Well, it's like this," he responded. "Heaven is interested in results." Then he paused. "When you preached, people just slept. But, when that man drove, people prayed!"

I smile each time I think of that little story. The fact of the matter is that, like heaven, we must be about getting results. The key question for our mentees should not be: What do you know? It should be: What did you do with what you know? What truth did you actually apply to your life? How did our mentoring experience change your life?

One of the key benefits of a good mentor is that they can facilitate growth and, yes, even life change. They help their mentee turn research into reality. They close the gap between potential and performance.

but how do we do it?

Since the goal of our mentoring should be life change, it is imperative for us to understand how change is best fostered in our mentee.

117

Once again, the most effective mentors and coaches in history are ones who built a system to bring about transformation in the people they led. Moses. Gandhi. Vince Lombardi. John Wooden. When I examine the annals of history, I am once again impressed with how Jesus of Nazareth did it. Like the others I just mentioned, He used a system that transformed the lives of His twelve mentees. Regardless of what you conclude about His identity, I challenge you to study Him as a mentor. His methods were stunning.

Each of these transformational mentors employed the Hebrew model of learning, as opposed to the Greek model. As I mentioned in Chapter 1, the Greeks had been "making disciples" for generations prior to Jesus's venture with His twelve men. Socrates mentored Plato; Plato mentored Aristotle; Aristotle mentored Alexander the Great and so on. But disciple-making to the Greeks was an academic exercise in which the mentor instructed and interacted with his students verbally. Their job was to receive the information. It was cognitive and cerebral. It was basically a transmittal of information and insight (philosophy) through the Socratic Method. The Hebrew model was much more experiential. It was more than information; it was transformation. They would experience life together as a model and an observer. It involved doing, delegating, discussing and debriefing. It was active.

Granted, the fastest way to transmit information is verbal. It is the Greek model for learning. However, it isn't nearly as effective at changing a life. Students learn more effectively through observation and application than they do sitting in a classroom getting information. Both are necessary.

the big idea

As I study the Hebrew model in the pages of scripture, I see a pattern. There are four methods that were consistently used to equip mentees to embrace a principle. I believe we can summarize how this system fostered life change by taking the word "IDEA" and allowing it to serve as a reminder of how the Hebrew model can be employed today.

I – *INSTRUCTION* (We must teach and instruct our mentees verbally.)
While mentoring is more than mere talking, it does begin with conversation. We must introduce ideas and principles to our mentees and communicate them in a relevant way for them to understand them. Words furnish pictures and parameters for ideas.

D – *DEMONSTRATION* (We must provide a model for them to observe.)
It isn't just about words, however. Mentoring is not about telling but show and tell. Most people appreciate a model. They want to see it in action. The greatest management principle in the world is: People do what people see.

E - *EXPERIENCE* (We must let them participate and apply the principles themselves.)
Watching and observing is great, but it still doesn't guarantee life change. Most people won't incarnate a principle into their lifestyle until they get to experience it firsthand themselves. Mentors must allow them to practice it.

A - *ASSESSMENT* (We must debrief our time with them and evaluate their progress.)
Finally, experience is not enough, and I don't believe it is the best teacher. I have seen students have a bad experience and draw a wrong conclusion. I believe mentors must provide a place to evaluate and debrief what they have experienced.

Obviously, utilizing this strategy will require you to do more than just talk at your mentee. Again, words are helpful, but life change happens more permanently when we:

- Help them through KNOWING
- Help them by SHOWING
- Help them to get GOING
- Help them see their GROWING

Why not discuss the topic of public speaking or planning an event for instance? Share your struggles with them as well as your victories. Tell them what you've picked up over the years. Then, why not take them with you to an event to watch you do it? Later, why not push them out of the nest (at the right opportunity) to try it themselves while you observe? Finally, why not sit down and evaluate what was learned through the experience? Assess their growth and progress; correct the mistakes; debrief what they learned and hold them accountable to continue in it.

In a nutshell, the process can be crystallized by the following age-old process:

> • WE DISCUSS IT
> • I DO IT, YOU WATCH
> • WE DO IT TOGETHER
> • YOU DO IT, I WATCH
> • WE DEBRIEF
> • YOU REPEAT THE PROCESS WITH SOMEONE ELSE

If we mentors will practice this beautiful model, as best we can, we'll find our mentees undergoing transformation. At least that has been my experience. I've seen the pitiful results when I've failed to do this; I've seen the powerful and positive results when I've successfully done it.

jonathan's story

I mentioned my daughter's thirteenth year in the last chapter. My son is four years younger, so he had to wait for his mentors. During his thirteenth year, we decided to plan his year of mentors a bit differently. I met with five other dads who all had sons about the same age, all of them in middle school. We determined we could provide a much more EPIC experience if we worked together. So, we took a year and met with our sons twice a month, focusing on building them into "champions" (the word is an acronym, with each letter standing for a virtue we wanted to build into their lives). We tried to practice the BIG IDEA, providing words, examples, experiences and evaluation.

For instance, when we talked about life-planning, we took them to a local airport and met with Dan Cathy, the president of Chick-fil-A restaurants. He is also a pilot, who took the boys up in a jet and gave them an amazing experience in the air. He did the zero-gravity thing and explained how a jet operates, from take off to landing. Later, we met in a room at the airport and talked about how a flight plan is much like a life plan. No pilot takes off without a flight plan. No person should enter their adult years without a plan either.

Throughout the year, we introduced these young students to great men. They met famous men in the world of sports, such as Tony Dungy and Kyle Petty. They met a Marine colonel. They met musicians. They met pro athletes. They met business owners, pastors, mountain climbers and school teachers. Each exposed the boys to a new experience and an unforgettable lesson.

At the end of the year, we held two significant meetings. One was just for us dads and sons, where we presented them with a new name and action figure, drawn by a professional artist. Then, we presented them with a sword and held a knighting ceremony. It was a night they will never forget. You should have seen those boys with their swords.

The final meeting was for friends and family. We invited between 200-300 people to come and witness the boys' rite-of-passage ceremony. In front of the witnesses, we showed a video of highlights from the year together, we gave them a baton, symbolic of the fact that we dads are passing the "baton" of manhood to them. We read them each a personal letter, expressing how much we believed in them and their future. We gave them each a plaque to hang on their wall, and we surprised them with a personal letter from the president of the United States, which encouraged them to be leaders for America in the future. Needless to say, my son won't soon forget that year.

paving the way...

What prepared Jonathan for that year was a trip we took just prior to the experience. I let both of my kids choose a place they wanted to visit when they turned twelve. Each could pick anywhere in the world and travel with me to see it. Once there, we would have fun visiting sites together, but the trip would end with some meaningful talk-time.

Jonathan chose Minneapolis, Minnesota. I know it may sound strange, but at the time, he was into Camp Snoopy at the Mall of America, and there was a particular show that was playing in that city he wanted to see. So we did both of those gigs.

On the last day of our four day trip, I told Jonathan we were going to drive up near one of the lakes in the area. We weren't going to do the mall or a show. He knew something was up and wasn't sure if he liked it. I pulled into a parking lot in our rental car and stopped next to the water. Then, I turned to my son and gave a bit of a shock. I said, "Jonathan, let's trade places." I paused. "I want you to get behind the wheel of this car and drive around the parking lot a bit."

He was stunned, especially because he is a bit of a rule-keeper. "Dad, no! I am only twelve. I can't drive." I smiled and encouraged him that I would only have him drive around the parking lot for a few minutes.

"Dad, I can't. I am not big enough. This isn't good. Mom will not like this, dad. Mom will not like this!"

When I finally talked him into it, he slipped into the driver's seat with fear and trembling. He slowly backed out, trying to imitate all he had seen me do over the years. Soon, it became fun for him. He's a boy, and like most boys, driving a car eventually became natural and enticing. He was actually quite good at it. I had to stop him after a few minutes. It was after this experience that a meaningful conversation ensued.

I said, "Jonathan, how did you feel when you first took the wheel?"

He was honest. He acknowledged that he was panicked. Terrified that he couldn't do it. Then, I said, "But you found out that you could it after all, didn't you?"

When he agreed, I went on. "Jonathan, those feelings are exactly what you'll be feeling as you enter manhood. You will think you can't do it; you don't know what you are doing but you won't want anyone to know how you're feeling. Being a man is a lot like taking the wheel of a car. You are no longer a passenger in life. You are a driver, and you are responsible to get to a destination and to get the passengers in your car safely there as well. Growing up means become a driver instead of a passenger (it is one of the Habitudes® I will share in chapter twenty).

Next, we drove over to a graveyard, where we walked among the gravestones for several minutes in silences (Jonathan thought it was morbid at first). Afterward, we talked about the words that were on the tombstones. Single phrases described the people buried in that graveyard. They each got just one sentence. After reflecting on them, we began to talk about the sentence we would want others to remember us by. What would our sentence be if we just got one? It was a profound conversation, even for a twelve year old.

That trip involved conversations, experiences, examples and evaluation. I tried to use the big IDEA as I communicated the principles I hoped my son would remember. Now, years later, it is fun to observe him. He has remembered that year well.

people empowered for the task

As you know, when tradesmen train apprentices, they do more than just hand them a job. They empower them as leaders. We, too, must learn to empower others in our colleges, businesses, churches and spheres of influence. This involves the belief that knowing the mechanics of life and leadership is not enough.

To empower simply means to give your power to someone else. Empowered mentees usually emerge only when someone else has intentionally walked alongside them, investing in and developing them through demonstration and application. One who empowers has made a commitment to a person, a process, and a purpose that results in the building of an anointed change-agent in the lives of others.

As A Mentor You Empower When You...
- Know yourself (your areas of strength).
- Know your mentee (their areas of strength).
- Clearly define the goals and assignments.
- Teach the "whys" behind the principles you share.
- Discuss "process items" with them.
- Spend relational time with them.
- Allow them to watch you in action.
- Give them the resources they need as they act.
- Encourage them to journal through their experience.
- Hold them accountable for their actions (gain permission to do this).
- Give them the freedom to fail.
- Debrief and affirm them regularly.

the requirements of empowering

There are some fundamental requirements for the mentor to empower a mentee. The following ingredients are the non-negotiables.

1. RELATIONSHIP AND TIME
2. BELIEF IN THE PERSON
3. LOVE EXPRESSED THROUGH LISTENING
4. DISCERNMENT OF NEEDS
5. DEMONSTRATION OF MINISTRY
6. PRAYER FOR GRACE/HOLY SPIRIT
7. AWARENESS OF THE PROCESS

the results of empowering

1. THEY BECOME CONFIDENT (Security)
2. THEY BECOME COMPETENT (Ability)
3. THEY BUILD CHARACTER (Integrity)
4. THEY BECOME A CHANGE AGENT (Influence)

Another great word for empowering is the term "developing." I believe the highest aim we can pursue with mentees is not simply to shepherd them, nor even to equip them for ministry. It must be to develop them to be what they're gifted to be and do: managing deals with immediate care for their needs, reacting to their cry for help, equipping deals with proactively preparing them for a task, developing deals with growing a person to not only mature and serve, but to multiply as well. Note the chart:

EMPOWERING PEOPLE		
MANAGING	EQUIPPING	DEVELOPING
Care	Training for service	Training for personal growth
Immediate need focus	Task focus	Person focus
Relational	Transactional	Transformational
Service	Management	Leadership
Labor	Labor by addition	Labor by multiplication
Immediate	Short term	Long term
Feeling better	Unleashing	Empowering
Availability	Teaching	Mentoring
Focus on nurture	Focus on specific work	Focus on specific leader
No curriculum	Curriculum set	Curriculum flexible
Need oriented	Skill oriented	Character oriented
Maintenance	Doing	Being
What is the problem?	What do I need?	What do they need?
Problem focused	Purpose focused	Person focused
They begin to walk	They'll walk the first mile	They'll walk the second mile

exhibit 15-1

When we commit ourselves to develop our mentees, we will not only change a life, we will also have a friend for life. No other investment of our time even touches it. Developing people is strategic, it is multiplicative, and it's the highest expression of value for a mentee.

incurable optimism

Let me summarize this chapter by saying that if we're going to empower our mentees, we must develop an incurable optimism about them and about the future. We must possess zeal for people and for tomorrow.

Early one morning in a crowded elevator, a businessman became annoyed by another's cheerfulness. "What are you so happy about?" he growled.

"Well, sir, I ain't never lived this day before!" came the reply.

No one else in the elevator had either, but the one who had the optimism and perception to see the possibilities of the new day became, for a brief moment, a mentor to the rest. Such quality of life cannot be taught, only caught.

Frank Lloyd Wright had it. At the age of eighty-three he was asked which of his architectural works he would select as his most important. He replied, "The next one."

Viktor Frankl, who spent years in a Nazi concentration camp, had it. He noticed that those who believed in tomorrow best survived the day. Those who believed that tomorrow would never come were those who did not survive.

The prisoner who had lost his faith in his future was doomed. With his loss of belief in the future, he also lost his spiritual hold: He let himself decline and become subject to mental and physical decay.

Anne Sullivan had it. A classic example of a mentor/teacher, she was engaged by the parents of Helen Keller to teach their blind and deaf seven-year-old child. On March 3, 1887, in Tuscumbia, northern Alabama, she began her mission that would astonish the world. On March 20, 1887, Miss Sullivan wrote:

"My heart is singing for joy this morning. A miracle has happened! The light of understanding has shone upon my little pupil's mind, and, behold, all things are changed.

125

The wild little creature of three weeks ago has been transformed into a gentle child; she is sitting by me as I write; her face serene and happy, crocheting a long red chain of Scotch wool."

This belief or faith in tomorrow is eventually translated into the life of the mentee. The mentor's authority carries weight enough to transmit optimism to the mentee. We must stay committed to encouraging our mentees until they possess the ability to encourage themselves. Positive affirmation is necessary because of the consistent onslaught of negative input our society gives to mentees.

The late Dr. Nathaniel Bowditch was a captain who led a number of ocean voyages through dangerous waters. As early as age 21, he sailed an East Indian voyage and began to feel the weight of mentoring the young sailors on board with him. He knew most of them would be nothing but sailors all their lives unless someone began to invest in them and train them to go beyond their job descriptions. He painstakingly began to instruct the entire crew of the ship in the art of navigation. He shared all he knew with those rugged seamen despite the expense of time and sleep. The results were extraordinary. Without exception, every sailor on board during that voyage later became the captain of a ship. Needless to say, that's a rare occurrence. But such are the natural consequences of associating with a man who senses the responsibility of making deposits in others and whose generosity earns a position of authority in everyone he contacts.

Fran Tarkenton, former Minnesota Vikings quarterback, once called a play that required him to block onrushing tacklers. NFL quarterbacks almost never block. They're usually vastly outweighed by defenders so blocking exposes them to the risk of severe injury.

But the team was behind, and a surprise play was needed. Tarkenton went in to block, and the runner scored a touchdown. The Vikings won the game. Watching the game films with the team the next day, Tarkenton expected a big pat on the back for what he'd done.

It never came.

After the meeting, Tarkenton approached coach Bud Grant and asked, "You saw my block, didn't you, Coach?" How come you didn't say anything about it?"

Grant replied, "Sure, I saw the block. It was great. But you're always working hard out there, Fran. I figured I didn't have to tell you."

"Well," Tarkenton replied, "If you ever want me to block again, you do!"

Don't ever take your words lightly. Sometimes, little words can transform the way a mentee lives. May I suggest you review this chapter often? It is central to the task of mentoring, because mentoring is all about changing the life of a mentee. Practice the truths listed here and your influence will expand.

Over the last thirty years, I have endured more than my share of problems, challenges and failures in mentoring. Regardless of how much experience I tucked under my belt, new people seemed to always bring new struggles each time a mentor relationship was formed. Every time I mentored someone, it seems I found new mistakes to make.

Two of my personal failures stand out to me. Perhaps reading about what I learned from them will encourage you. The first took place in 1985. I was supervising the internship program at a large church in southern California. During that year a very real schism occurred between two of my interns: It was a division that, on the surface, appeared to center around their philosophical and theological differences. I hesitated to step in between them, wanting to allow them to resolve it as adults. By the time I did intervene and determine a solution, it was too late to salvage one of those relationships. Sean, one of these two young men, was deeply hurt. Out of his pain, he had rallied twenty-five to thirty others who became sympathetic to his perspective. Angry and bitter at my decisions over the issue, Sean left the church, taking the group of twenty-five with him.

Looking back, I now can see that differences in theology weren't the issue. Sean had no father. His dad had left their family years earlier. He'd perceived my hesitation and subsequent decision as one more rejection of him by an authority figure. It appeared that I had taken sides with the other intern. I sat down with him and sought his forgiveness for my leadership failure.

I now wish I had taken initiative sooner (i.e., been more proactive), I wish I had exercised deeper discernment (i.e., been more perceptive), and I wish I had defined the values and goals of our ministry more clearly (i.e., communicated priorities). It hurts me to think how unnecessary this struggle really was.

My second big mentoring failure happened right in my home. Arriving home late one evening, I entered through our garage door expecting to find my wife, Pam, at the door to greet me. She wasn't there. I searched the house, only to find she had already gone to bed. When I leaned over to see whether she had fallen asleep yet, I received quite a shock. She was wide awake with tears streaming down her cheeks. Tissues were scattered around her pillow. She had been there a while.

Immediately, I shifted into high gear to fix whatever problem was troubling her. I raced through my mental files hoping to figure out what could be wrong. I was clueless. Finally, I asked, "What's wrong, honey? What happened today?"

She lay still for a moment. Then, she responded quietly, "That's just it, Tim. Nothing happened." I was still in the dark. I asked her to continue. I am sure what she said next hurt her more than it hurt me — and it was horribly painful for me.

"Tim, you're doing such a great job leading the people at the church," she whispered. "Everyone loves you. And, I don't want to stand in the way of that..." She paused. "But, no one is leading our home right now. Nothing is happening in our family, and I feel alone and forgotten. I feel like I have nothing more than a roommate who is busy."

Those words shook me up. We both cried for the next forty-five minutes. And on that evening, I realized I had failed as a mentor — in the life of the person I cared for most. I had neglected priority one. As a pastor, I had blundered in my service to my number one parishioner! With fresh resolve, I made and have maintained a commitment since that evening: If I mentor no one else the rest of my life, I will invest myself in mentoring my wife and two children. Again, more lessons in discernment, initiative and priorities.

the most common problems
No doubt, you, too, will experience some tough moments as you attempt to mentor someone.

Simply because both of you are human means you'll face some hurdles before the race is over. Along the way, you will notice that there are recurring themes in those hurdles you face (I certainly did!). You will observe that certain problems surface again and again in human relationships. It has been my experience that four problems emerge as the most common ones between mentors and mentees. Let me list them for you here:

1. Unmet Expectations
2. Relationship and Personality Clashes
3. Failure to Meet Objectives
4. Inability or Unwillingness to Act and to Multiply

Although mentoring difficulties may take on a thousand different shapes and sizes, these four primary categories summarize the majority of them. In this chapter I would like to address each of these briefly and provide at least some basic guidelines for you as you seek to resolve them in your own mentoring journey.

unmet expectations

Probably the most common struggle for Generation Y, when it comes to authority and organizations, is unmet expectations. Both the baby boomer and the baby buster have grown up with TV and slick marketing, which promises the world to them by noon, tomorrow. Generation Y has all that marketing but in more forms than ever. If Generation X struggles with authority, Generation Y struggles with reality.

This has led to disillusionment within the young adult population. They are disappointed at how often promises are broken and at the lack of integrity leaders seem to possess. They are savvy to the false excuses we have given them. They don't need us for information — they get it online before we do. They need our integrity. When you combine the unrealistic expectations the media fosters in them along with the oral and character failure of many leaders within corporate America (Enron, Tyco, WorldCom, etc.), you can see we have a real problem on our hands.

Frequently, however, their expectations are unmet because they are unspoken. Young and old alike bring emotional baggage to a mentoring relationship that you, as a mentor, have no idea exists. Recognizing this, it is good to employ the Principle of Pro-activity:

131

**It is better to build a fence at the top of the cliff
than a hospital at the bottom.**

The more problems you can resolve before they ever arise, the better off you will be. Let me recommend the following "fence-building" techniques that will enable you to address your mentee's expectations.

1. *Clarify the precise purpose at the beginning of your relationship.*
   Don't leave anything to chance. Give time for both of you to express your "big-picture" goals and desires for the mentoring relationship — up front. Before you ever open up a workbook to study or determine a book or article to read through, talk over your purpose for meeting. I usually invest the first two meetings together to nothing but getting acquainted and defining expectations in this way. Remember, results in mentoring are birthed from relationships.

2. *Ask them the top three results they want to gain, from being mentored. This step breaks down the bigger picture of step one.*
   Ask them to bring a list of items they consider key result areas with them to your next meeting. I generally write these three items down and repeat them back once they've finished articulating them. Sometimes I'll even make this list into an "agreement" both of us sign, acknowledging that we'll focus on those items in our times together.

3. *Explain your limitations of time and ability.*
   Take the time to elaborate on how much you realistically can do as a mentor. Sometimes, a mentee wants a second father, and they become resentful when you fail to fulfill that need in their life. Admit to them that you are human. Then detail for them where you believe you are strong and weak in your mentoring experience. This will obviously require you to be secure and emotionally stable, but if you can do it, it will pay off big time. Agree to a relationship that you know you can satisfy in their life. Discuss the kinds of needs you both can meet for each other.

4. *Inquire about their past experiences with authority.*
Their answer to this question may disclose priceless information to you. Have they struggled with authority figures in their past? What is their relationship like with their dad? How about their teachers or professors? How about former pastors? You get the idea. I began mentoring a young adult years ago, only to discover that they had a huge chip on their shoulder when it came to anyone suggesting how they live their life. We endured some painful conflict that we could have avoided had I known their track record.

5. *Converse regularly about your mutual goals and expectations.*
As you continue meeting together, spend time talking to each other about how you are doing. Remind them of your original goals. Decide you will have a consistent feedback time and communicate if the relationship is bearing the fruit you had hoped it would. Remind them of your desire to meet their needs. Make sure they are convinced you have their best interests in mind.

As a mentor, you will want to model right attitudes and appropriate expression of emotion, especially concerning your own unmet expectations. Very likely, there will be times when your mentee will let you down. Keep this list in mind as you seek to help your mentee in the relationship process.

relationship and personality clashes
A second common hurdle we must jump as mentors is often over looked at the beginning. I am speaking of personality conflicts with our mentees. Someone once said about marriage: "We fall in love with our spouse's strengths, but we marry their weaknesses." The same is often true about a mentoring relationship. There are certain qualities that draw us to a partner or mentee, but it isn't until later that we discover just how human they really are! Just as in marriage, we do not discover these relationship struggles until we're in the midst of the commitment.

five options
The fact of the matter is we ALL have warts and wrinkles. In addition, friction always occurs at some point if two people are trying to make progress toward a goal. I have found we are faced with five options, we all face when we get into a sticky relationship conflict. We can respond in one of five ways:

133

1. **I'LL GET THEM!** *(We choose revenge; to retaliate and get even)*

2. **I'LL GET OUT!** *(We choose escape; we break it off and avoid them)*

3. **I'LL GIVE IN!** *(We choose to surrender and let them have their way)*

4. **I'LL GO HALF!** *(We choose to compromise and meet halfway)*

5. **I'LL DEAL WITH IT!** *(We choose to address the issue in a healthy way)*

we must remember...

- *Conflict is Natural.*
  (It is going to happen because of our human differences)
- *Conflict is Neutral.*
  (It is neither destructive nor constructive in itself)
- *Conflict is Normal.*
  (It happens to all of us, strong or weak; you are not alone)

The following steps are a short-course on conflict management.

1. *Compliment*
   Begin by focusing on their positive qualities. Affirm those characteristics that first drew you to your mentor or mentee. Dr. John Maxwell calls this the 101% Principle: Find the 1% you agree on or like about them and give 100% of your attention to it!

2. *Compromise*
   Admit early that you are willing to assume some responsibility for the conflict. Recognize the differences in motivation and style, depending upon your temperament (i.e., sanguine, melancholy, phlegmatic or choleric personalities). Determine that you will give in to a degree and meet them halfway. Compromise may be a good solution.

3. *Choice*
   Next, layout the choice that stands in front of you both. You can either flee it, fight it or face it. Determine, if at all possible, to address it and take any steps you can to make the relationship work. Remember the axiom: Friends may come and go in life, but enemies accumulate. Relationships will dissolve unless you work to cultivate them.

4. *Challenge*
Extend a clear challenge that they can respond to and maintain their dignity, if possible. Remember, it is more important to win the person than to win the argument. Layout good parameters and boundaries you feel are appropriate to make the relationship work.

5. *Confidence*
Finally, end by expressing your sincere confidence in them. Let them know you trust them to make the right decisions and that no personality conflict will prevent you from loving them and caring about their future.

Ann Kiemel Anderson used to repeat a little poem years ago as she described the countless times she found herself in a conflict with someone, or simply wanted to reach out to a person with their "walls" up. It goes like this...

he drew a circle
He drew a circle that shut me out, heretic, rebel; a thing to flout;
But love and I had a will to win, wo drew a circle that took him in.

One last word on this subject. In order to preclude personality clashes, I recommend that you use a "Mentor Profile." This is simply a form which potential mentors and mentees can fill out, indicating their hobbies, interests, personality type, goals, motivational needs, leadership style, spiritual gifts, etc. Then, as mentors are matched up with people, you can place people together that seem to fit relationally.

I have provided a sample of my "Mentor Profile" in Chapter 19, which is entitled: "How Can I Help My Organization Begin Mentoring?" Feel free to modify this form to suit your own organization.

failure to meet objectives
This is the third common problem in mentoring. For me, this is the toughest of all mentoring problems. It revolves around the mentee's failure to accomplish a task or assignment, keep a promise, maintain a proper attitude, finish a lesson or, ultimately, to become what you both agreed they would become — a mentor themselves.

Let me begin to respond to this problem by communicating some further "fence-building" steps you can take to prevent this dilemma before it even happens:

135

1. *Have both the mentor and mentee sign a formal covenant together.*
   This may sound "cheesy", but it has saved many from crashing and burning in their commitment to mentoring. Both partners can sign a sheet that expresses their commitment to finish the process, including all of the agreed upon assignments (I have provided a sample Covenant in Chapter 19. Feel free to use it or modify it to fit your personal tastes).

2. *Write down the specific, detailed assignments you expect to complete.*
   Before you begin, make a list of the tasks or assignments in which you might want them to participate. You may not be able to predict all of them, but you will certainly help the mentee get "psyched up" for what lies ahead.

3. *Consistently remind them that life is the summation of our choices.*
   We are all guilty of saying, "I just didn't have the time to do that!" The reality is that we didn't make the time. We all have time to do what we believe we must do or want to do. Stephen Covey said it best: The issue is not prioritizing your schedule, but scheduling your priorities. We choose what is important and valuable to us, and the best indicators of those choices are our calendar and our checkbook.

4. *If necessary, you may need to push the "pause" button on the experience.*
   On a rare occasion, I have had to suspend a mentoring relationship because they established a pattern of neglect. They just weren't able or willing to meet the objectives. We could either pretend all was well or we could face the fact that we were not doing what we said we would do. When this happens, there is an "elephant in the room." We all know it and someone needs to bring it up.

I had one such instance where I postponed a mentoring experience with a college student. I apologized that I was asking him to do too much at that point in his semester. He felt relieved that I was allowing him to step out of the commitment and follow through on it later when he was ready. One year after we suspended the mentoring experience, he felt ready to pick it back up, and everything went well the second time around.

the bottom line

You may remember Chapter 13 of this book, entitled, "How Do I Confront Effectively?" In that chapter I walk through the steps I take when I need to confront a failed objective, a sin or bad attitude. I want to encourage you to review those steps I give in that chapter as a guideline for your own confrontation. Do your best to embrace these additional principles when meeting with your mentee to confront their failure:

1. **BE A GRACE GIVER.** All of us need to be believed in, and we never need it more than when we have failed to keep a commitment. Affirm them most as a person when you feel they deserve it least.

2. **DISCUSS THE "WHY" BEHIND THE FAILURE.** It may help for you to guide them in their discovery of why they couldn't fulfill an expectation. Was it inability or unwillingness on their part?

3. **SEPARATE THE PERFORMANCE FROM THE PERFORMER.** Don't connect their failure with their person (i.e., they failed because they are a failure!) Always criticize the performance, not the performer. Failure is an event, not an identity.

4. **DEVELOP A PLAN TOGETHER TO PREVENT REPEAT FAILURES.** Sit down with a pad of paper and create a game plan for the future. If they have a pattern of failing at a certain task, help them to develop a new pattern.

5. **STAY TRUE TO YOUR CONVICTIONS.** In your empathy, don't compromise what you know is right. The assignment was a good one. Applaud conduct based on character (i.e., doing what is right), not based on feeling (i.e., I felt like doing it).

6. **HOLD THEM ACCOUNTABLE.** You may be the only one in their life who will take a stand and not let them off the hook of their commitments. Once you've spelled out the goal, talk to them about it consistently. Hold them to finishing what they start.

inability or unwillingness to multiply

The ultimate problem or difficulty we face as mentors comes when our mentee fails to apply the truths they learn. In other words, failing to reproduce what they've experienced with you is an abortion of the ultimate goal!

We don't mentor others just so they can feel better about themselves, but for them to grow and turn around to multiply; they are to pass on what they have received. When they refuse to do this, it is a crime in my book!

consider this: If we do not enable our mentees to go full circle so that they can repeat what we have done with them, we have at least partially failed. Remember, leadership is always just one generation away from extinction. Each generation must mentor the willing people of their own time period. Success without a successor is a failure. A true disciple will become a disciple maker.

what you must do

There is no fool proof answer to this dilemma. If there were, someone would have packaged it, sold it and made a mint years ago. However, there are some initial steps you can take to preclude this problem. Once again, I direct you to some fence-building action items for the future:

1. *Talk about multiplication and reproduction from the beginning.*
   Don't allow your mentee to even begin the process with you without knowing that the expectation is to multiply. They should understand that this is the price tag of receiving so much of your time. Tell them outright that you are assuming they will pass on to their own mentee what they receive from you.

2. *Find creative ways to discuss it throughout your mentoring experience.*
   Don't limit your discussion of this subject to the beginning of your mentoring relationship. Like any vision or conviction, your vision for leader reproduction should be communicated consistently and repeatedly. I believe we must:

   - SEE IT CLEARLY
   - SHOW IT CONSTANTLY
   - SAY IT CREATIVELY

3. *Locate the stumbling blocks that would prevent multiplication from happening.*
   Each of us has different reasons for our inability or unwillingness to mentor others. Mentoring is all about relationships. Hence, in this step you must probe the heart and head of your mentee, in cooperation with them, and discover why they find it difficult to obey:

- What are their fears?
- What are their weaknesses?
- What is their track record/past experience?

Once you have put your finger on why they seem paralyzed you can help them effectively. Then, you can proceed with discussion on a game plan that could enable them to overcome the stumbling block.

going deeper

I believe that if you practice the suggestions and truths I communicate in two other chapters in this book, you will successfully defeat this enemy and overcome this obstacle. I'm going to ask you to review the content of the following two chapters:

1. **Chapter 17:** *How Do I Enable a Mentee to Become a Mentor?*

2. **Chapter 19:** *How Can I Help My Organization Begin Mentoring?*

don't assume anything

In Chapter 19, I explain how you can set up a structure for mentoring relationships to be fostered and empowered. My research shows that without a helpful system for mentoring, 95% of the people that are mentored will never go on to multiply. People need structure. We generally don't admit this. In fact, we usually project just the opposite. We say we don't like structure, at least not too much structure. It's too confining, too limiting. Indeed, I'll be the first to admit it can be. I have seen churches who squelch creativity and individuality because of the "sacred" programming in the church. However, in our effort to escape this extreme, we retreat to the other end of the spectrum. We offer no system for developmental relationships and fail in our efforts to multiply!

Even if your mentee promises to find a mentee and replicate your investment in them, the majority of the time they will fail to keep that promise. Unless they are in the unusual top 5% of the typical population, they will find themselves unable to follow through for some reason. Most of the time it is due to human infirmity and lack of accountability.

The system I advocate is one which I saw work effectively at the local church where I worked for eleven years in San Diego. I didn't create the system, although I wish I had.

It is a system promoted by small group and discipleship gurus all over the world. I have simply modified to fit a mentoring ministry. It involves selecting a Point Person to oversee the ministry. Then, as mentoring relationships come to a close, the graduating mentees qualify to become part of a Mentor Cluster in the church. They are now ready to mentor someone else and join this cluster, even before they may have found their own mentee. This provides ongoing input, encouragement and accountability to reach the goal of multiplication and continued growth.

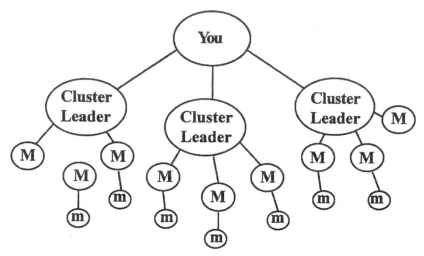

exhibit 16-1

mentor clusters

As I mention in Chapter 19, don't be afraid to start small. Do not relish only big enterprises. In fact, don't prefer small ones or big ones. We should celebrate growing ones because growth is a sign of life.

This structure will enable you to grow the mentoring initiative where you are. It will allow you to take it beyond just one generation. It might empower you to leave a legacy.

I trust that the answers to the problems in this chapter will furnish you with a springboard to your own answers. Remember, the reason you endure the hardships we've discussed in this chapter is because mentors are committed to the next generation. If we don't pass on what we possess, others may not get it. We are building the future. Perhaps this poem says it best. It's called, "The Builder."

the builder

An old man traveling a lone highway came in the evening
cold and gray To a chasm deep and wide.
The old man crossed in the twilight dim,
The sullen stream held no fear for him,
But he stopped when safe on the further side
and built a bridge to span the tide.
"Old man," said a fellow pilgrim near,
"You are wasting your time in building here,
your journey will end at the close of the day,
You never again will pass this way,
You've crossed the chasm deep and wide
Why build this bridge at evening's tide?
The traveler lifted his old gray head,
And to his fellow traveler said:
"There followeth after me today
A youth whose feet must pass this way;
The chasm that's been naught to me,
To that fair youth may a pitfall be;
He, too, must cross in the twilight dim Good friend,
I am building this bridge for him."
~Author Unknown

I know it sounds quirky, but I was thinking recently about some of the most famous pairs of mentors and mentees. I thought of people like Batman and Robin. King Arthur and Sir Lancelot. Socrates and Plato. Moses and Joshua. Anne Sullivan and Helen Keller. Mr. Miaggi and Danielson. Johnny Carson and Jay Leno. Phil Jackson and Michael Jordan. John Wooden and Bill Walton.

What do they have in common? For many, the mentee was able to do what the mentor had done and more. Somehow the teacher was able to equip their partner to reach the standard they had set. Some of those mentees even soared beyond their mentor.

Everyone knows that a civilization only survives if the population living inside will reproduce. If the present generation fails to produce offspring, there will be no second generation. This is basic biology. It is also basic leadership development. Species reproduce after their own kind. Dogs beget dogs. Cats give birth to cats. Humans give birth to baby humans. And only leaders can reproduce other leaders. If they fail to do this, a new generation may not get to enjoy following healthy leaders.

the joshua problem

One of our Habitudes® is called, "The Joshua Problem." Habitudes® are simply images that form leadership habits and attitudes.

Four thousand years ago, the greatest Jewish leader in the world was a man named Moses. If you've never read about him, my guess is you've seen the movie. Cecil B. DeMille directed the classic film decades ago called, The Ten Commandments in which Charlton Heston played the role of Moses, the Patriarch of Israel. It was unforgettable.

In the story, Moses leads the people of Israel out of slavery in Egypt, through the wilderness, right up to the banks of the Jordan River. At this point, he stops. He doesn't finish the job of taking the Hebrew population into the "Promised Land." He is old and gray and ready to die. Fortunately, for several years Moses had equipped an apprentice named Joshua. Once Moses passed away, Joshua took the reigns of leadership and led the people across the river into the land flowing with "milk and honey." He was ready for the job and consequently, the nation of Israel didn't have to slow down one step as they crossed the Jordan and claimed the land. Although it took years, one by one, they entered the cities and began to settle. Thank God Moses had a "Joshua" to finish the job he was unable to complete.

The problem was: Joshua didn't have a Joshua. As far as we can tell from the reading of Scripture and other contemporary writings, Joshua never duplicated the gift Moses had given him. He never took a young leader under his wing and prepared him to lead. Sadly, when Joshua died, Israel entered the worst period of her history — the period of the Judges —where twice we read this statement:

> *"And there was no king in Israel in those days and*
> *everyone did what was right in his own eyes."*
> Judges 17:6; 21:25

Why is it we see this dilemma — this Joshua Problem — repeated thousands of times each year in organizations around the world? I don't know if leaders are just lazy or ignorant or shortsighted, but many of them last one generation then leave their teams in shambles, wishing their leader was still around. As we ponder changing the culture we live in, our first consideration must be the development of next-generation leaders. Leaders are carriers of the culture. I believe we must be biased toward leader development. Unless we are, we'll take the easy route and focus on our tasks at hand. The "urgent" will replace the "ultimate." Dwight Moody once said, "It's better to train a hundred men than to do the work of a hundred men. But it is harder."

turning a mentee into a mentor

Releasing a mentee to become a mentor is the crux of our labor as mentors. Before we examine how this is done, let's define what we're aiming for and why. Let's attempt to grasp the vision for leader-reproduction.

the truth and the myth

Let's first dismantle the myths about mentoring and disciple-making with a protégé. Contemporary culture has confused three areas of everyday life with this art of mentoring.

MENTORING IS NOT...

MYTH #1: EDUCATION

It is not simply the implanting of information for the sake of knowledge. While education is great, mentoring goes beyond lectures, drills and testing. The "stuff" that has changed the world generally involves action not merely mental gymnastics. It isn't about a vast education or accumulation of knowledge. It's often servanthood, commitment and purpose. It is about attitude as much as aptitude.

MYTH #2: FRIENDSHIP

While friendship does occur, we've often confused fellowship with mentorship, hoping that just getting people together will do the trick. If that were true, we would have millions more influential leaders. People are getting together all the time. Mentees don't need to know what leadership looks like in the school building or the church building, but rather out in the real world. And...it must be intentional.

MYTH #3: MEMORIZATION AND DRILLS

While some of our mentoring or may include memorizing and studying facts, it cannot be the crux of it. Intellectual exercises and disciplines aren't enough if our lives don't change. Mentoring is about doing what we know to do. We were never meant to know more than we do. As I have already stated, it is about closing the gap between potential and performance.

MENTORING IS...

TRUTH #1: THE ORIGINAL LEARNING METHOD

Dating back thousands of years, mentoring is a life-on-life method for passing on wisdom, experience and values to a new generation.

It is designed to accelerate the progress of mankind, so a new generation doesn't have to repeat the mistakes of the previous one. It is what Socrates did. It is what Confucius did. It is what Jesus did.

TRUTH #2: PARENTING

To mentor or disciple someone will remind you of the parenting process. This does not mean you are to mother the mentee. What I am saying is that you must invest your life in them. It is more than the transmittal of facts. In scripture, the Apostle Paul even described himself as a father and mother to the Thessalonians in I Thessalonians 2:7-9.

TRUTH #3: MULTIPUCATION THROUGH REPRODUCTION

We must understand that adding to the population will never be enough if we're going to transform the world. World impact requires multiplication. If nothing else, the birth rate of the world's population teaches us this. We must multiply leaders through life-on-life reproduction. What happens biologically must happen relationally with leaders.

each one mentor one

Dr. Frank Laubach's epitaph reads:
"The man who taught the world to read"

Dr. Laubach popularized the phrase "Each one teach one." By his simple four-word strategy of teaching one illiterate to read under the condition that they would teach another to read, several million people have now experienced the thrill of reading for the first time. The chain continues to this day, long after his death.

try to imagine...

Pause for 60 seconds right now and try to imagine the implications of the mentoring relationship. What if you stopped fretting over changing the whole world this year, and focused on a few? What if each leader, over a lifetime, mentored just 12 people?

> You mentor 12...who mentor 12 equals 144!
> ...who mentor 12 equals 1,728!
> ...who mentor 12 equals 20,736!
> ...who mentor 12 equals 248,832!
> ...who mentor 12 equals 2,985,984!

is an unbroken chain of mentors realistic?

Probably not, but the point is clear. Even if only a small fraction of mentors and mentees follow through, an extremely significant difference in the number of leaders in the twenty-first century would be made. Today, the future governor of your state or the future president of our nation may be in your scout troop, your athletic team, your class at college or youth group at church.

Multiplication brings exponential growth. The gentleman who created the game of checkers understood this. Years ago, this inventor was summoned to visit the King (he resided within a monarchy), and he was thanked for the game. In fact, the King offered him vast riches in his Kingdom in exchange for it. The inventor thought for a moment and then made his request. He asked for one grain of corn for the first square on his checkerboard, two for the second, four for the third, then eight, then sixteen, then thirty-two, etc. It was exponential increase. But the King didn't see it. He was livid with anger over such a small request. Little did he know the amount of corn required to fill the last square was such an enormous number — his Kingdom didn't even have that much corn! That's the power of compound growth. Multiplication isn't glitzy, but it sure beats addition in the end.

why we dropped the ball

So, what happened to us? Why do we fail to practice this simple but profound act of investing our life and wisdom into a handful of others? I believe there are a myriad of reasons. Let me suggest just a few big ones below.

1. **HUMAN NATURE**
   We migrate toward comfort zones and the path of least resistance. It is easier just to hold big lectures and host big meetings than to invest the emotional energy in a mentee.

2. **PROFFESIONAL VS. LAITY DISTINCTION**
   We began producing professional teachers and preachers who had all the answers; the laity became "ignorant audiences." The Latin root word for "laity" is the word "idiot."

3. **INSTITUTIONALISM**
   The schools, learning centers, colleges and churches became cold, sterile, impersonal corporations. Professionals were paid to do this kind of work in an academic building.

147

4. THE GREEK LEARNING MODEL
Schools and churches embraced an academic, passive, educational model instead of the Hebrew model of developmental relationships.

getting started
As you commit yourself to the multiplication of leaders through mentoring, consider the following sequence of steps:

1. *Study to "own" a conviction and vision for mentoring.*
   Don't try to export what you don't own first. Take the time to own the vision for this.

2. *Select a person or group from your following to be a mentee.*
   Identify people in your circle of influence who already know you and respect you.

3. *Cast vision to them for multiplication (they will mentor someday).*
   From the beginning, talk about them taking what they learn and passing it along.

4. *Ask for commitment from your mentee.*
   Don't wait to ask for the commitment you want. Be up front with expectations.

5. *Be prepared and set goals (create lesson plans).*
   Don't wing it in your meetings. Like a good teacher, prepare objectives and lesson plans.

6. *Meet regularly for a set time.*
   I suggest you have a set time to start and finish. If you wish to continue, you always can.

7. *Apply the principles and lessons together.*
   Don't just talk. Practice the principles together and debrief what you discover.

8. *Invest yourself in the person and process.*
   Be sure to see the steps your mentee needs to take in order to grow over time.

9. *Help them find a potential mentee.*
   Once you finish, work with your mentee to select and challenge their own mentee.

10. *Evaluate and launch them to try it themselves.*
   Don't end without taking some time to evaluate their growth; empower them to multiply.

you just might change the world

It's true. Making a commitment to take your mentee full circle and reproduce another leader could change the world. It certainly did with Jesus and the twelve. It has also happened various times through history. John Wesley founded the Methodist church on this principle. Even in the twentieth century, movements have begun when men have mentored in this manner.

Dawson Trotman is a beautiful example. "Daws" was the founder of The Navigators, a worldwide nonprofit organization committed to mentoring and training men and women in the Navy. Early in his career, a young sailor named Les Spencer approached Daws and asked for help with personal growth. Daws clarified that what the sailor was really asking for was to be mentored or discipled. He then agreed to do it over the next several months. During the experience, this sailor's life was so dramatically changed that he brought a buddy of his to Daws and asked if Daws would disciple him as well. The reply startled both of the sailors: "Absolutely not." Then, Daws went on to say, "If your friend is going to be discipled, it will have to be you who does it." So the two of them connected in a developmental relationship. Upon their completion, the chain continued. Both went out and found someone in whom they could invest their lives. This happened again and again and again.

What makes this story so intriguing is that it literally transformed the atmosphere on the ship. The Commanding Officer became alarmed at the "new" crew he had on his hands. Eventually, the F.B.I. was called to investigate what was going on. Some thought a cult had broken out. Others wondered about the odd behavior of what was once a normal group of sailors. Clearly, things were different. What's more, once the F.B.I. began to investigate, it took them four months to sift through all the men who had been mentored in order to find Daws — the one who had started the whole thing.

It is interesting to note that by this time, it was late in 1941. Do you remember what happened in December of 1941? Pearl Harbor was bombed, and the surviving sailors on board those ships were scattered everywhere — and the Navigator organization went global.

149

That is one thick web of mentees! What an encouraging snapshot of what could happen if we became serious about multiplying. We must remember, however, that leadership reproduction happens one life at a time. Be committed to starting a movement as opposed to a program. Programs usually start big then fizzle and become small. Movements usually start small and become huge. Movement leaders in history have collected a tiny group of mentees and, after pouring their life into them, pushed them out of the nest to fly. The world has never been the same since.

I think those leaders had the right idea.

The good news about mentoring is that it can be done somewhat effectively at a distance. Mentors don't have to live nearby, nor do they even have to be alive to speak into our lives today. Yes, you read that correctly.

Through the consumption of books, particularly biographies, we can be mentored by the greatest leaders from our past. Some books, wrote Francis Bacon a century ago, are to be tasted, others to be swallowed, and some few to be chewed and digested. Worthy books are like mentors — available as companions and as solitude for refreshment. Thomas Carlyle, in his essays, noted that if time is precious, no book that will not improve by repeated readings deserves to be read at all. I've set a goal to read two books each month, and I can't imagine my life without the companionship of these faithful mentors.

A book is good if it is opened with expectation and closed with profit. The books you choose say much about you. Don't be a one-issue reader. Read widely, even books by authors with whom you disagree. Taste some, chew some and digest the best.

Abraham Lincoln's life illustrates beautifully the value of books as mentors. These storehouses of knowledge carried him through disappointments that would have shattered a weaker man. Among the troubles that visited him were the death of his mother when he was only nine, rejection by his first love, the bankruptcy of his first business venture, defeat the first time he sought public office.

Even when he finally made it to Congress, he lasted only one term, being so unpopular that re-election was out of the question. At that point in his life he told a friend, "I will get ready. My time will come."

Remember Abraham Lincoln when you look at your protégé and are tempted to give up. I can't think of a better expression of faith than, "I will get ready. My time will come."

how to benefit from biographies

My good friend and colleague Steve Moore shares the following insights regarding mentors from the past.

Historical role models provide us with a source of passive mentoring from which all of us may benefit. Regardless of our circumstances, we can surround ourselves with brilliant thinkers, creative visionaries and hot hearted radicals by reading biographical accounts of great leaders from history.

It is how we approach the reading of these works and what we learn from them that is important. Exciting true events unfold within the covers of biographies. However, entertainment should not be our motivation for reading them. Neither should we look at these leaders as antiquated players in history, relevant only to their time and location. We need to evaluate their lives from various perspectives with the intention of learning practical lessons that will empower us to become world changers today. Here are some pointers gleaned over the years on how to benefit from biographies.

1. **Maintain a perspective as to where the mentor fits in history.**
   Disassociating historical mentors from their place in history robs us of an important sense of perspective. Questions about the sociopolitical climate of a historical mentor's world need to be answered in order for us to meaningfully process the events of their life. It is usually helpful to construct a leadership time line and develop the historical setting out of which the timeline arises. A leadership time line might include a series of phases such as foundations, inner-life growth, career-service and maturity. The length of each phase will vary and might span a decade or more. Such a time line would include important events in the individual's life as well as important historical events. This will allow you to evaluate the impact history had on the person as well as their impact on history.

For example, when William Booth became consumed with the launch of the Salvation Army in London, during the late 1800s, it is important to note the horrific conditions of the inner city of London during that time. The industrial revolution was peaking and both children and adults were being taken advantage of by manufacturers and factories. The poor were everywhere, and there was no organization systematically caring for them. William and Catherine felt they had to do something about the great need of their day.

2. **Read with a sense of purpose; know what you are looking for.** Identify the process items of each stage in the historical mentor's time line. Process items include the ways and means that fostered a person's climb into leadership. They may be events, people, circumstances, interventions or inner-life lessons (if you would like to know more about the term "process item," read Robert Clinton's book, The Making of a Leader). Look for clues to their leadership style, how they implement change, deal with failure or opposition. Make note of their methods. Were they innovators, reformers or pioneers? Did they make extraordinary sacrifices or face difficult suffering?

For example, Harry Truman was a geek growing up on a farm. He would have been voted the least likely to become a leader as a kid. He wore thick glasses and seldom left his father's side on the property. He left for college but had to return home because of his dad's failing health. He was the only president in the 20th century to fail graduating from college. It was during his service in World War I that changed everything. As his troop rode through Europe, the Germans began dropping something from the sky. Everyone scattered in fear; Truman's horse fell on top of him. But when he saw his comrades running in fear, he hopped up and yelled at the top of his lungs for them to come back. They had not finished their mission. Everyone was shocked that such passion lived inside of young Harry Truman. Later in his journals, Truman wrote that he learned two things about himself that night: First, that he had a little courage. Second, that he loved to lead. Harry Truman went on to become president of the United States and made perhaps the toughest decision of the century: to drop an atomic bomb on Japan.

3. **Become a member of the historical mentor's inner circle.**
Most great leaders get close to only a handful of people. The higher up the leadership ladder they climb, the more inaccessible they become to the broad base of their constituency. But through a biography you can literally move into the inner circle of leaders who surrounded a historical mentor. You can sit in on board meetings, listen to private conversations, read personal letters and journal entries!

Just imagine you were given the opportunity to spend a week with John Adams, Thomas Jefferson, Franklin Roosevelt, Mother Teresa, Chuck Colson, Joan of Arc, Billy Graham or the leader of your choice. You could not ask questions — only follow the leader and observe them — at home, in the office, on the road, wherever they go. Would you do it? Of course you would! Future generations will probably get this opportunity by way of biographical writings. But you can access the inner circle of hundreds of great leaders, not just for a week, but for the better part of a lifetime.

4. **Identify important windows of opportunity in the historical mentor's life.**
In the developmental stages of most leaders, there are a few key windows of opportunity through which the primary focus of their ministry is opened. Much can be learned from identifying and evaluating those key moments. How was this mentor prepared for these opportunities? How long did they prepare? Did they have a sense of destiny regarding their career focus? How rapidly did their vision unfold after the windows of opportunity were opened? What were the key factors in their decision to take new steps of faith? Did they know early on what their role in history would be?

5. **Identify the historical mentor's ultimate contribution.**
The term, "ultimate contribution" comes from the studies of the leadership emergence theory under Dr. J. Robert Clinton. An ultimate contribution is defined as a lasting legacy of a person for which they are remembered and which furthers the cause for which they worked, by one or more of the following: setting standards for life and service; impacting lives by enfolding them or developing them; serving as a stimulus for change; leaving behind an organization, institution or movement that serves as a channel to positively impact the world; or the discovery or promotion of ideas — communication that furthers a vision or movement.

154

category: presidents in history

When evaluating the lives of historical mentors, there are scores of potential categories for ultimate contributions. A specific research project identified twelve primary categories for ultimate contributions or lasting legacies from the lives of U.S. presidents. These twelve categories are listed in the following chart.

ultimate contribution/ lasting legacy	thrust of contribution
Model	living a quiet, yet model life of integrity
Stylistic Practioner	demonstrating an effective, timely leadership style
Mentor	productive development of individuals
Public Rhetorician	productive inspiration among large groups
Crusader	right wrongs and injustices in society
Artist	creative breakthroughs
Founder	starts new organizations
Stabilizer	solidifies organizations
Researcher	develops new ideation
Writer	captures new ideation for the use of others
Promoter	distributes effectively new ideation
Pioneer	founds innovative entrepreneurial type works

Keep in mind that there will likely be some overlap between these categories, and most leaders will make more than one ultimate contribution.

Keep a quote on file that summarizes a main principle you have gleaned from the historical mentor. Many people have read biographies of great leaders but can remember very little, if anything, about them. One of the best ways to glean the most from historical mentors is by collecting quotes that summarize a key principle from their lives. If you do not actually memorize a quote, try to at least learn the details of an important vignette from the historical mentor's life.

It is helpful to write down a quote and share it with other people for several months as a means of reinforcing it. While you are learning the details of a vignette, share them with others for as long as it takes to lock them into your memory.

155

some lasting examples

In 1996, I wrote a book called The Greatest Mentors in the Bible. In it, I attempted to summarize what we can learn today from the mentors found in the Hebrew culture and written up in scripture. I found thirty-two mentoring relationships in the Old and New Testaments — from Abraham and Lot, to Jethro and Moses, to Naomi and Ruth, to Paul and Timothy. Clearly, we can learn from each of these relationships and gain some handles for our lives today.

Some ten years later, our organization (Growing Leaders, Inc.) created a mentor training kit, called: "Lifelines — Becoming the Life-Giving Mentor Your Students Need." In it, I interviewed a number of current mentors and discovered they, too, embraced a set of historical mentors who had long since passed away. It became clear to me that history is loaded with people who can teach us, in different styles, from different methods, connecting with different personalities for different purposes — if we will only let them.

This is my point: Mentors are everywhere, past and present. We can be mentored by any leader — even those in history who have long since past away — if we'll let them speak into our lives and influence the direction we are heading. In order to do this, we must approach them as mentors, not just stories from past. I challenge you to do just that.

Many of you who read this book or use it as a reference guide, long for your school, organization, business or church to begin a formal mentoring initiative. You have thought about it and even prayed for it. You wish someone would lead the way. You're convinced, deep down, that if people would just commit themselves to this kind of developmental relationship, lives would change and so would the atmosphere of your group.

I have some good news for you. I agree. Furthermore, in this chapter I will lay out some guidelines for you to pursue this lofty vision. I must warn you of something, however. If you apply the material you are about to read, it will force you to think big! It may even cause you to re-examine your own values. Your hunger for mentoring may have begun with a self-serving purpose — you knew you needed a mentor. I am going to challenge you to think beyond your own needs now and focus on your team, college, church or whatever organization you're a part of right now. I want you to ask yourself: "What realistic steps could I take to facilitate a mentoring initiative that might impact the next several generations?" Once you pondered that question, you are ready to begin. Let me share some tips I think will enable you to participate in a successful launch.

what has not worked on the campus?

Let me first give you a 35,000 foot fly-over of what is working around the U.S. and what is not working, in terms of mentoring programs with young people. The following statements are drawn from surveys asking what is NOT working on college campuses:

1. Programmed relationships containing too much structure.

2. Mentoring relationships that are exclusive faculty to student match ups.

3. Mandatory mentoring for the entire student body.

4. Information-based meetings centered around the transmittal of content.

5. Mentors unleashed with no preparation or equipping.

6. Campus wide mentor programs launched without buy in from a core.

what has worked on the campus?

In contrast, these statements were taken from surveys to discover what IS working on college campuses today:

1. Student-to-student mentoring involving upperclassmen helping underclassmen.

2. Mentors launched after quality training experiences to prepare them.

3. Adult to student relationships including staff and alumni as mentors.

4. Mentor programs funded by alumni.

5. Mentor programs begun by a core of committed people who model the experience.

6. Mentoring relationships with clearly defined goals and deadlines.

the necessary ingredients

Let me remind you to not get discouraged about "starting small." As you consider helping your organization begin a mentoring initiative, probably the worst thing you could do is insist that it begin with a huge, organization wide "blow-out" rally where everyone is encouraged to jump in and get involved. This is how we envision and evaluate successful new programs. May I remind you, you're not starting a program; you are on the front end of a movement.

Remember my words early in this book: Programs usually start big and then fizzle when their novelty has waned. Movements usually start small and grow very big because they begin at a grass roots level and grow organically. Gandhi began a movement with just a handful of people. William Wilberforce began a movement with a handful. Dr. Martin Luther King Jr. began a movement, which at its peak only had 1% of the U.S. population. Jesus began a movement with twelve men, not a program with 12,000, and changed the world. Please hear me. It is best to begin small, with a committed core of people.

When bakers begin the process of baking a cake, they usually take a gaze at the list of ingredients they will need. They get the big picture of what they are getting themselves into before they turn the oven on. We ought to begin the same way. The following are the ingredients I believe you'll eventually need to launch a good mentoring initiative.

1. *A Point Person.*
   Someone will have to offer leadership, cast vision and own the responsibility for helping the initiative get off the ground. This person is the key spokesperson for the vision. They must live and breathe mentoring.

2. *A Mentoring Structure or System.*
   While mentoring may begin with just a handful of loosely knit people, it will not continue to grow unless you implement some kind of structure for people to enter. This system will enable things to continue after you're gone.

3. *A Vehicle for Enlisting.*
   I suggest you design a "Mentoring Match-up Form" for all persons who want to sign up for mentoring. This form will help prevent relational "train wrecks" and improve the chances of success. I provide one later in this chapter.

4. *A Written Commitment that People Agree Upon.*
   Mentoring is a broad subject. There must be unity around the vision. You will invite chaos and disappointment unless you develop a "covenant" people can read and sign to know what they are getting in to.

5. *A Healthy Approach.*
Finally, you must take the right approach in order to see this movement get off the ground. Your approach to a new idea can make it or break it. At the close of this chapter I will suggest some healthy steps you can take.

Let's take a look at each one of these ingredients, one by one. I will do my best to give you samples or suggestions of how each one can be achieved.

a point person

Dr. John Maxwell has said, "Everything rises and falls on leadership." Even if you feel that statement is an exaggeration, you could not argue that most of the success of any team or organization rests on the vision and credibility of the one who leads it.

This illustrates vividly how important it is for the right point person to be selected for this new mentoring initiative. Ideally, they should have the desire and ability to take charge. They should have favor with the people, particularly the potential candidates of the initiative itself. They should know how to communicate vision (a little charisma wouldn't hurt). They should have a vision to think beyond one generation of candidates, and they should be willing to pay the price to set this initiative in motion. First gear always requires more work than fourth gear. Momentum may be our best friend, but building it often takes hard labor!

The point person would ideally be an influencer within the organization. They should be perceived by the people as credible and worthy of following. It is helpful for them to be well liked and respected. When they speak, people listen. J. Oswald Sanders provided us with the greatest one word definition for leadership when he said: Leadership is influence. Period. This is the optimal point person profile. Look for such a person, and don't eliminate your self from the list of possibilities!

I mentioned one of the fundamental truths of mentoring earlier in this book when I said, "We teach what we know, but we reproduce what we are." Because this is true, you must be careful in the selection of this point person. The people who enlist in the initiative will begin to reflect the personality and values of the leader. The initiative's bandwidth, its flavor and speed, its attraction and reputation will almost all be dependent on the person who spearheads the operation.

For this reason, may I suggest an acrostic for the point person and every other leader who participates in your mentoring ministry? Mentors are PROVIDERS. They provide for the mentees who watch and follow them. Hence, I believe the word PROVIDER will serve as a terrific job-profile for this point person. Note the following qualities:

A MENTOR POINT PERSON MUST BE...

P – *PURPOSEFUL*
From now on you can no longer be casual about the people and relationships around you. Because there are people following, you must live and serve on purpose, not by accident.

R – *RELATIONAL*
Sometimes this doesn't come naturally, especially if you're task-oriented. However, because mentoring is about relationships, you must learn to model healthy relationships.

O – *OBJECTIVE*
As a leader or mentor, you cannot afford to allow your personal tastes to interfere with doing what is right. You must objectively assess people, relationships and mentor match-ups.

V – *VULNERABLE*
Another area you must model is the area of self-disclosure, transparency, honesty and relational vulnerability. Our mentees are going to emulate our level of openness.

I – *INCARNATIONAL*
Incarnation means "to become flesh." A mentor or point person cannot merely talk the talk, but must exemplify the kind of life and ministry they desire from their followers.

D – *DEPENDABLE*
Regardless of your past inconsistencies, from now on you, as a leader, must be absolutely dependable and responsible to those who work with you and under you.

E – *EMPOWERING*
You must take on a style that is empowering to those around you. To empower means to give your power away. You must delight in and facilitate the successes of your followers.

R – *RESOURCEFUL*
Perhaps above all, you must be resourceful with every tool God has given you. For the progress of the vision, use wisely every person, dollar and opportunity you have.

One more thought: This point person does not need to emerge from the very beginning, although that would be helpful. He or she must simply step forward or be chosen by the time your organization is ready to communicate the vision to a larger constituency and go public. At this point, someone must assume responsibility for the health and development of the movement.

a mentoring structure system

The second ingredient that must be included in our recipe is a system that will facilitate a growing population. As I mentioned earlier, most of us attach a negative connotation to the word "structure" or "system." The words sound confining, like they might squeeze the breath out of the vision. However, if you read the great leaders in history, you'll find, almost without fail, that they worked a strategy. There was a method and a plan once the original leaders saw the vision catch on.

Consider this: You will only grow your initiative to the size of one person unless you create some structure that invites other people into it. In fact, I will suggest you need structure for the following reasons:

- You want the initiative to expand and grow, to reach many people you may not know.
- You don't want to lose track of who and where each mentor and mentee is serving.
- You want each person to stay involved and begin mentoring after they are mentored.
- You want new people to enter the initiative easily and in an organized fashion.

If you agree with the statements above, then keep reading. I would like to introduce a system to you that is relational yet organized. It is one that places mentors in small groups for support and accountability, and it exemplifies the Hebrew learning model in the process. Let me show you the diagram I introduced to you earlier that illustrates how this system looks:

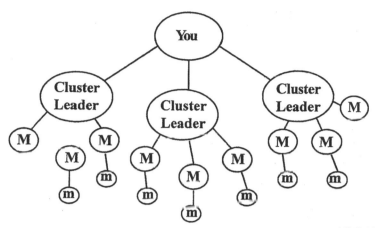

exhibit 19-1

In the diagram, you see words and letters. The large circle with the word "YOU" in the middle is the point person. The circles with the words "Cluster Leader" are the facilitators of mentoring clusters. These cluster leaders are really mentors to the mentors. They meet with the mentors once a month for support and accountability. These clusters are ideal not only to provide on-going training and input for current mentors, but also for mentees who've just finished being mentored and now need some consistent encouragement to reproduce. The capital letter "M" is for the mentors who are in the cluster. Each of them is attached to a mentee (one to one or small group), who is signified by the lower case "m." Mentors meet with their mentees as often as they choose: weekly, bi-weekly, etc.

In short, you may begin with just two or three mentors meeting with their mentees. But as the population grows, you select cluster leaders to coordinate graduating mentees and current mentors, meeting with them monthly for support and accountability. I suggest you put no more than six to eight mentors per cluster since it would be difficult for a cluster leader to manage more than that number. The goal is: Once anyone is finished with their mentoring relationship, they are placed in a mentor cluster. Obviously, the more mentors you have, the more clusters and cluster leaders you need.

You can quickly see that the point person and the cluster leaders are all strategic selections. If you find good nurturing leaders to head up the clusters, you will likely have a successful, ongoing mentoring initiative.

163

Before moving on, let me share some final words of encouragement regarding this system. I have seen it work in several locations across the country. It has worked best when the following action steps were included:

1. *Have your clusters meet with their cluster leaders in homes.*
   It's usually a warmer, more relaxed atmosphere than the office building, campus classroom or church.

2. *Serve food.*
   Food always helps break down any relational barriers. Light snacks that can be consumed while you are discussing issues are ideal.

3. *Meet regularly.*
   A rhythm of meetings that is predictable is optimal, such as the first Monday night of the month, etc. Do your best not to disrupt this rhythm.

4. *Be sure the cluster leader is well prepared for each meeting.*
   Remember, they are the mentors for the mentors. Each meeting ought to be excellent and provide incentive for the mentors to show up, whether it's the friendships, the training, the support, etc. You may want to discuss issues relevant to mentors, like confrontation, motivation, listening, etc.

5. *With the direction of the cluster leader, consider good match-ups for the new mentors needing to find mentees.*
   Wise counsel often comes from such a group of experienced people.

the leadership development process

At Growing Leaders, Inc., we use a leadership development process to illustrate the stages people grow through in their journey. Note the diagram on the next page:

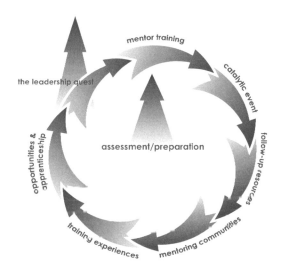

Notice, it begins with assessing where the organization is now. How healthy is the culture? How ready are the people for a mentoring initiative? What must be done to prepare the way? Next, I suggest you prepare the potential mentors. This can be done via a six to eight week training time or a pilot mentoring group, full of sharp, potential mentors. Once the preparation is over, these trained people can help launch the initiative.

The next step is a catalytic event. Along the way, you will want to expose the larger population in your organization to the mentoring initiative. When you are ready to do this, we've found it helps to host an event (or conference) where you cast vision for mentoring and leadership development. At the conclusion of the event, you can provide attendees the opportunity to "sign up" to join a mentoring community.

Once you know the interested people, you should choose the direction for these mentoring communities. This doesn't mean you have them all go through identical curriculum, but you choose a course that will deliver what the mentees need. The content they will discuss is only a guide — not a god. The mentoring communities should meet for one semester or one year (four to twelve months). Once finished, these mentees can receive on-going training through the mentor clusters and begin mentoring and leading themselves. For more information on this cycle, go to: www.GrowingLeaders.com.

the three-step process

Other organizations choose to utilize three steps: events, small groups and coaching. It utilizes "small groups" as an intermediate step that allows someone to join a small group to simply discuss what was introduced at the event. This process that still leads people through a mentoring journey, but it fosters growth through three simple steps. Each step has a distinct purpose below:

STEP ONE	STEP TWO	STEP THREE
Catalytic Event	Small Group	Coaching/Mentoring
Motivation/Information	Reflection/Interpretation	Application/ Transformation

a vehicle for enlisting

The third ingredient you'll want to add to the recipe for a successful mentoring initiative is the creation of a vehicle for enlisting people. Once you've moved beyond the first generation or two, you'll be ready to invite others into the mentoring experience. One common challenge you'll face at this point is the matching up of potential mentees and mentors. How do you know they'll like each other? What if they don't sense good chemistry between them? Can you prevent relational "train wrecks" before they occur?

I believe you can help yourself immensely by creating a "Mentor Match-up" form for any person interested in getting involved, whether they'll be a mentor or mentee. This form allows them to put on paper their goals, personality and style, hobbies and interests, spiritual gifts, etc. in order to be placed with a compatible partner.

Whenever someone expresses an interest in being mentored or becoming a mentor, simply give them this form and put the ball in their court. You respond to them only after they have filled out the form. This will be one way to discover just how interested they really are.

Notice the sample form (Appendix B) I have provided for you at the end of this chapter. It can be typed and formatted easily on one 8 ½" x 11" page, front and back. Look it over carefully. It allows for a person to communicate whether they are looking for a mentor or mentee: their hobbies/interests, their motivational needs, leadership style, temperament, etc. Each of these answers can be obtained by taking the simple tests provided on the next few pages.

The results of each of the tests reveal information helpful to your matching them with the appropriate partner. For instance, note the following descriptions:

1. **Temperament Test** *(Appendix C)*
    This simple test, designed by Florence Littauer, lets you know their personality type. It is based on Hypocrites, the Greek philosopher, and his studies of the four major personalities: Sanguine, Melancholy, Phlegmatic and Choleric.

2. **Motivational Needs Survey** *(Appendix D)*
    These results tell you what motivates the person most: completing a task, relating with people or influencing a group. Each of us has different combinations of motivational needs that are good to know at the beginning.

3. **Strengths Finder Test**
    This test is available through the Gallup Organization. It reveals a person's top five strengths. These are helpful to know for career positions as well as interpersonal relationships. You can find these at: http://sf2.strengthsfinder.com/.

Be sure and have every person who fills out this Mentor Match-up form be as thorough as possible. The more you know, the better chance you'll have of placing them in the right mentoring relationship. The goals of the mentor and mentee should obviously match, but don't be afraid of putting opposites together, in terms of personalities, as long as they know you are doing this for the sake of their growth and development. Once you match two people together, suggest that they meet twice just to get acquainted and to see if they have compatible expectations and styles.

a written commitment that people agree upon

A fourth ingredient I've found helpful in the mentoring initiative is a written agreement or covenant that both the mentor and the mentee sign.

This covenant allows the two individuals to declare formally their intention to follow through and remain committed to the relationship and the goals laid out in the beginning. The covenant does not need to be elaborate, but should state the basic values and goals of the mentoring relationship. These are especially helpful with young people.

Every one of us has made a commitment in the past that we have failed to keep. It is frustrating. It can be embarrassing. This signed agreement empowers the parties to publicly become accountable to each other and the others in the initiative. It increases the likelihood of finishing what they started and reduces the drop-out rate. It is not fool proof, but it is the closest thing to fool proof you'll ever find with a group of volunteers.

Notice the sample covenant provided in Appendix 16-4. In addition to the actual covenant, I have also provided a list of possible covenant guidelines in Exhibit 16-5. This could be handed out to each person who will sign the covenant as a confirmation of the values and common ground rules everyone has agreed to follow.

a healthy approach

The final ingredient our recipe calls for is a healthy approach. This means you will initiate your approach to this mentoring initiative in the organization in a mature way and in full submission to the leaders in that organization.

It could be very easy to do "end runs" around the established leadership, especially if they don't share your passion for mentoring. Don't do it. Be patient. Slow down if you need to, but don't play the role of the renegade or maverick that bulldozes over everyone in the way. You cannot force this idea into being. You and the leadership must work cooperatively. This is the optimal method for the future health of the vision.

No doubt, the practice of mentoring can make a big difference in your organization, campus or church. However, it may not do so right away. It should generally start at the grass-roots level, with one or two mentors investing in one life at a time.

My suggestion would be to begin small, but plan some infrastructure for mentoring to continue as new generations of people finish being mentored and go on to mentor someone else. Consider the following list as a sequence of steps:

1. Study and work for you and your organization to own the vision for mentoring.
2. Define the commitment and plan on paper (both short and long term).
3. Obtain the approval of the leadership in your organization.
4. Select a person or group from your sphere of influence to mentor.
5. Invest in your mentee: the person, process and purpose.

6. Challenge your mentee to multiply (reproduce) when they finish.
7. Train and release your mentee to challenge their own mentee.
8. Choose (or become) the point person for the mentoring-initiative.
9. Develop a form for mentor match-ups.
10. Establish a structure for mentor clusters (see earlier chart).
11. Create a system for interested people to sign up.
12. Find places to communicate the vision to the larger population.

As you can see, this practical list of twelve steps includes each of the ingredients I have listed earlier. I am recommending that you follow this list in the basic order I have given it. If you find it difficult to wade through these steps alone, find a confidant who can provide some emotional support as you pioneer and implement this vision

Don't forget that the journey of a thousand miles begins with a single step. Blessings on you as you step out and begin to influence so many others, through mentoring.

There are a variety of tools and resources you can use as you mentor others. Along the course of your relationship with a mentee, you may decide to read through books together, review articles, meet people in the community or listen to CDs and watch DVDs to foster discovery.

One tool we want to introduce to you is a series of small books called: Habitudes®. Habitudes® are images that form leadership habits and attitudes. Each book contains thirteen images that teach life and leadership principles through the power of images, stories, questions, assessments and practical exercises. As far as I'm concerned, they are the easiest and stickiest way to get a student to learn and remember truths that will impact their life. Everyone loves pictures, and pictures spark conversation.

consider this. We live in a culture rich with images. We grew up with photographs, TV, movies, video, MTV and DVDs. We can't escape the power of the visual image — and most of us don't want to.

I've learned over my career that most of us are visual learners. We like to see a picture, not just hear a word. Author Leonard Sweet says that images are the language of the 21st century, not words. Some of the best communicators in history taught using the power of the metaphor and image — from Jesus Christ and His parables to Martin Luther King Jr. and his "I Have a Dream" speech during the Civil Rights movement. "The best leaders," writes Tom Peters, "...almost without exception and at every level, are master users of stories and symbols."

the role of a HABITUDE®

Why? Because pictures stick. We remember pictures long after words have left us. When we hear a speech, we often remember the stories from that speech, more than the phrases used by the speaker, because they painted a picture inside of us. They communicate far more than mere words. In fact, words are helpful only as they conjure up a picture in our minds. Most of us think in pictures. If I say the word "elephant" to you, you don't picture the letters: e-l-e-p-h-a-n-t. You picture a big gray animal. Pictures are what we file away in our minds. They enable us to store huge volumes of information. There's an old phrase that has stood the test of time: A picture is worth a thousand words. I believe it's true. One of my undergraduate degrees was in commercial art. It was then I recognized the power of the image. Now I get to combine the power of teaching leadership truths with the power of pictures. I like to express my passion for each group who studies and practices them: I hope they linger in your mind and heart. I hope you discover layers of reality in them, as you grow. I trust they'll impact you profoundly as they have me.

These Habitudes® books make up a series, designed to furnish images you can discuss in a mentoring community. I encourage you to go through the series in a group. Each picture contains layers of reality, and your discussion can go as deep as you allow it to go. The books are created to guide you on your leadership journey. They are based on the fact that leadership isn't merely one-dimensional. It runs 360 degrees. We influence others all around us. We must first lead ourselves. Then, we will also influence those above us. Next, we will influence those around us. Finally, we influence those for whom we are responsible. Book One covers self-leadership. The journey should always begin here. Once I lead myself well, others will be magnetically attracted to follow. Influence naturally ripples from strong character. I won't have to force others to follow me.

The themes for each of the books in the series are:
1. **Book One:** *The Art of Self Leadership*
   (This book is about developing character, discipline, identity, responsibility, time management, etc.)

2. **Book Two:** *The Art of Connecting with Others*
   (This book is about hosting healthy relationships, conflict resolution. listening, encouragement, etc.)

3. **Book Three:** *The Art of Leading Others*
(This book is about positively influencing others, vision, planning, passion, priorities, initiative, etc.)

4. **Book Four:** *The Art of Changing Culture*
(This book is about how to transform organizational culture or even the culture of a community).

Some sociologists describe this generation as EPIC: Experiential, Participatory, Image-driven and Connected. If that's true, I believe we'll get the most out of resources that give us an image, an experience and a way to connect with each other. Each of these books provides you not only with an image, but a handful of discussion questions, a self-assessment and an exercise in which you can participate. Dive in and experience each one of them. My hope is that they become signposts that guide you and warn you and inform you on your leadership journey.

how do habitudes® help me as i mentor?
The Habitudes® series is a simple, profound way to connect with students and teach them character and leadership. They are being embraced by a number of corporations across the U.S. and internationally, but their greatest potential for impact lies in using them with next-generation leaders. Here is why...

1. *They enable you to teach leadership in a simple and brief period of time.*

2. *They can spark discussion that goes as deep as the maturity of your students.*

3. *They provide an image, relational discussion and an exercise to participate in together.*

4. *They offer you a set of transferable concepts that students can teach as well.*

5. *They are a series of four discussion guides based on a 360-degree leadership proposition.*

6. *They furnish you with a shared language for your leadership culture.*

If you want to make your mentoring times more memorable, and provide handles to your mentee as you share, then these Habitudes® might just take you to the next level. They seem to transcend cultures and age groups and even contexts.

Today, there are a variety of groups discussing the Habitudes® curriculum, including NCAA athletic teams, government leaders in Washington D.C., Fortune 500 companies, professional baseball teams, military officers and administrators, the Future Farmers of America, church youth groups and hundreds of schools across the U.S. and around the world.

To learn more about Habitudes®, just go to:
GrowingLeaders.com/Habitudes

Enjoy the journey.

It is in this final chapter that we get down to the brass tacks. We will discuss the goal of the mentor and exactly what we should do in the meeting with our mentees. I'll do my best to give you the big picture and the feel of a typical meeting. I want to speak in an especially practical and personal fashion with you in this final section. I dedicate this chapter to the purpose of enabling you to get the very most out of your mentoring experience.

setting up the meeting

Stu Weber, author of *Locking Arms*, writes about "the buddy system." He remembers his days in elementary school, as well as his days in the military, where he learned to use and appreciate the buddy system. This is simply a system of support and accountability where everyone in the group finds a partner and sticks with them. When his army sergeant told the troop to find a buddy, he remembers that he and most of the other guys in formation would have preferred jumping off a cliff, doing fifty push-ups or running ten miles in full battle gear. Later, however, he saw that the buddy system probably saved a number of kids' lives in school and a large volume of soldiers in Vietnam.

The point is that all of us need to find a "buddy" and take initiative to stick with them! I have found that the mentor in a relationship usually has to give permission to the mentee to set up their meetings together. Hence, in the beginning, the mentor must take initiative. After a few weeks, however, the mentee ought to exhibit enough "hunger" to pursue his mentor and take initiative to set up the meetings. Both will have to determine the frequency.

The meetings you have with your mentee should be held in a comfortable and safe setting. By safe, I mean an atmosphere where honest, transparent discussion can occur. As you ask each other personal questions, you will want to envision how safe you both will feel about conversing out loud about certain issues in public places. Accountability is best implemented in private.

If you are conversing over a "principle" and an assignment, I would suggest you begin by discussing the principle first, then its application. If the assignment is one that the two of you can do together, by all means do so. This may require your scheduled meeting that week to be out on a university campus where you'll be modeling good people skills or in a solitary place where you can create a budget together. The goal is simply that you think through the best possible place to dialogue and to accomplish life change.

the meeting

Once you sit down to meet, take initiative to set the tone and atmosphere. Ask about their week and take a few moments to review their personal life. Don't just jump into the "business." If you're prone to skip to the "business" just remember that their life is the business and the reason why you meet.

I've found it wise to begin the process with an initial meeting or two to clarify expectations on both sides. I ask them to list three goals or expectations that they would like to get out of the experience. Then I verbalize three of my own expectations or goals for them. I also attempt to convey the depth of my commitment to them. I cast vision for the potential I see in them and where they could go — if they want to. All of this lays a solid foundation for your subsequent meetings.

asking the right questions

As you think through the big picture of your discussion together, perhaps the little acrostic of SALT will help you follow an appropriate flow of dialogue:

S- *SAY SOMETHING AFFIRMING* (You are a Host)

A- *ASK THE RIGHT QUESTIONS* (You are a Doctor)

L- *LISTEN WELL* (You are a Counselor)

T- *TURN THE DISCUSSION TO THE TRUTH (PRINCIPLE) TO BE LEARNED* (You are a Tour Guide)

As you ask the questions, keep in mind that this may be your primary role in the meeting. The student may simply need you to probe like a doctor examining a patient. Doctors are always good at poking and prodding their patients during a physical examination to see "where it hurts."

an inductive approach

This probing and prodding is another way of describing the inductive approach to the art of mentoring. In the same way that getting acquainted is best accomplished through probing inductively to see where the common interests are in the other person, so it is true with mentoring. We should not approach our mentee with a package that we plan to jam down their throat whether they like it or not. That is the deductive approach. Instead, we must observe and diagnose what the issues are, then begin to address them. Again, this will require you to master the art of asking questions. That's what you must become proficient at doing. Your questions may flow best in this order:

highlights
- What were the highlights of the lesson/assignment for you?
- What stood out in your mind or made the biggest impact?
- What was the number one truth you learned from this lesson or assignment?

struggles:
- What were the chief struggles you had with the topic?
- Did you have any internal battles with the assignment?
- Do you have any barriers in your life that keep you from practicing the topic?

opportunities:
- What will it take to master this topic or issue?
- How will you attempt to implement the principle? (What new ways?)
- How can you further network with people/books to see life change in this area?
- In what ways could you and your goals advance if you practice this principle?

Asking these questions will end up being more profound than an eloquent lecture from you.

The reason is simply this: Asking questions encourages them to come up with and own the answers, not you. As you learn to "host" the conversation, you can guide them toward a healthy, effective response without just giving it to them.

Glen Urquhart and Bobb Biehl suggest some additions to this format when you want to simply discuss their personal goals. The mentee (or protégé) should come to the meeting prepared to discuss:

- A list of 1-3 upcoming *DECISIONS* to which the mentor can give perspective.
- A list of 1-3 *PROBLEMS* in reaching the protégé's goals to discuss with the mentor for help.
- A list of *PLANS* for the mentor's general information and update.
- A list of *PROGRESS POINTS* so the mentor is updated and can give well-deserved praise.
- A list of *NEEDS* for the mentor's wisdom, prayers and general support.
- Personal *ROADBLOCKS*, blind spots and fears the protégé would like to discuss.

drawing the right conclusions

Once they have distilled the proper conclusion or personal response, you will likely be the one to hold them accountable to make application. I always try to have a pen ready, and as they draw conclusions, I jot them down on a pad of paper and keep them in a folder under their name. Then I would begin this series of questions...

- Do you really believe and embrace the principle?
- How can I best hold you accountable to practice it?
- What could be your first step?
- When could you take it?

The point is not to press them into some performance trap, but rather to take them past mere intellectual assent into intentional practice. These lessons must go beyond mental gymnastics. And for most of us, that only happens when we are held accountable. Decide now to hold your mentee accountable in their obedience.

setting a goal for your mentoring

Obviously, it would be ridiculous to mentor someone without possessing a goal. We should always have the end result in mind when we meet with our mentee.

So what is the goal of our mentoring? What do we want our mentees to look like as the result of our investment in their lives? Good questions. These are the kinds of things you and your mentee ought to jot down in one of your earlier meetings. If you are mentoring someone in a business setting, you will set business related goals. If you are spending time on a school setting, obviously you'll want to set some educational goals. If you are serving in a church context, you may set ministry related goals. Context has a lot to do with both your goals and authority as a mentor.

hosting the discussion

One final reminder: Nearly every relationship and every conversation has both a host and a guest. I have drawn this conclusion after years of observation (this is another one of our Habitudes®). People seem to find their place in discussions as either the proactive guide (the host) or the responder (the guest).

These terms, "host" and "guest," are most often used in the context of a visitor to a home or party. A good host, upon opening the door and seeing the guest who's just arrived, will generally take charge and do certain things. They first say something like, "Won't you come in?" later they'll say, "May I take your coat?" and "Have a seat" and "Would you like something to drink?"

Each of these illustrates that the host is assuming the proper place of leadership, even if the topic of conversation is the choice of the guest. We all know how to be a good host without ever needing to read a book on it. The host is the relational leader by the mere fact that the context is on his or her home turf.

Within the mentoring relationship, I am challenging you, the mentor, to host the relationship. This does not mean you have to have the gift of gab or have something witty or profound to say on every subject. It simply means that you are the guide, making sure that the two of you get to your destination.

As the mentee calls you to set up the appointment, be as gracious as you can be. Welcome them into your life each and every time you make contact. As you invite them in, have questions ready, just as we discussed earlier. In fact, let me encourage you to enter each meeting armed with this arsenal:

- Have four or five questions ready
- Set your demeanor to be safe and affirming
- Decide that you will lead the way in being open and vulnerable
- Maintain a sense of the big picture — Where should you be leading this subject?
- Be ready to speak into their life concerning process items they must face

Review the principles in the chapter of this handbook called, "How Do I Speak With Authority into Someone's Life?" In that section, I review how to gain influence in the life of a student. My acrostic, again, is simply:

how to gain influence with people

I – *INVESTMENT IN PEOPLE*
N – *NATURAL WITH PEOPLE*
F – *FAITH IN PEOPLE*
L – *LISTENING TO PEOPLE*
U – *UNDERSTANDING OF PEOPLE*
E – *ENCOURAGER TO PEOPLE*
N – *NAVIGATE FOR PEOPLE*
C – *CONCERN FOR PEOPLE*
E – *ENTHUSIASM OVER PEOPLE*

It is my consistent prayer that you demonstrate these functions with your mentee. You are embarking on one of the most strategic endeavors of your life. You are now entering a labor of multiplication!

how one man did it

In early 1996, I read the biography of Charles Simeon as I worked on my doctoral degree. His was an amazing story about the power of mentoring. Charles lived during the latter part of the 18th century and into the early part of the 19th century. He was an Anglican minister who was about to give up on his work in the church because it seemed so lifeless and hopeless. Instead, he chose to simply focus on mentoring next-generation leaders across the street at Cambridge University.

He established a system whereby he would meet with students and form relationships with those who were hungry to grow and become leaders within the Anglican Church. He signed up to speak in chapel as often as possible. In his chapel presentations, he would challenge students to step beyond the status quo and become transformational leaders.

Upon finishing, he would invite those students who wished to go deeper, to a Tuesday night meeting that he called a "Conversation Group." During those Tuesday night meetings, he would take the interested students deeper and dialogue with them about the needs of their community. After those meetings, he would single out students and personally invite a handful to his house on Sunday afternoons to something he called "Supper Clubs." There he would mentor about twelve to fifteen young men who planned to graduate and become an Anglican minister themselves. He would talk about leadership and what it would take to serve effectively. Then, within the Supper Club cadre, he would isolate a few that were seniors and would soon graduate. He worked with them on the finer discoveries they would need to make upon entering the real world. Upon graduation, those young leaders were ready to lead.

Because the Church of England had a rule back then that allowed the wealthy parishioners to control who filled their pulpits by their donations, Charles Simeon was unable at first to place his graduates as clergy in the church. He didn't have the money. The one with the purse had the power. So, he decided to begin raising money in order place his trained mentees as leaders in those churches. He succeeded and soon had the funds to both train and position his mentees in places of service and influence.

Here's the amazing thing. Mr. Simeon did this quietly for fifty-four years. When he died, one third of all the churches of England were being led by "Simeonites" or mentees of Charles Simeon. He had made his mark on that nation, as an unsung hero, by the work of his mentees.

May others be able to say the same things about our lives when we're through.

it's your move

If you could have any Mentor(s) in the world...which person would you ask first, second and third?

1.

2.

3.

note: You may have three or more mentors at a time, each helping you win in different areas of your life (i.e., one spiritual mentor, one professional mentor, and one social mentor).

What three young people do you feel have the very highest potential for leadership...who may be open to your mentoring today?

1.

2.

3.

Start with one to three mentees first.

Start with one or, at the most, three mentees. When they grow to the point where they require less of your time and become capable of mentoring, you can begin mentoring others and so can they!

I believe the effort you put forth in mentoring others will be the best investment you will ever make!

appendix

The following pages represent tools to help you mentor. You will find assessments, forms and lists I mention earlier in this book. They are relevant and helpful items for mentors and mentees to connect more naturally. The assessments will help you understand your potential mentee and perhaps match mentors and mentees more effectively. In addition, you will find a covenant for mentor and mentee to agree upon and to sign. You will also find a list of resources to help you continue your growth as a mentor and as a leader who will develop other mentors in your organization. I trust these resources will deepen your impact as a mentor.

resources

The following are resources I think you'll find helpful as you practice the art of mentoring. They are a combination of books and kits for the corporate world, the student world and the faith-based world. Enjoy them as you fan the flame for mentoring inside of you and your organization.

A Hand to Guide Me
Denzel Washington / 2006 / Meredith Books

Mentoring: A Success Guide for Mentors and Protégés
Floyd Wickman and Terri Sjodin / 1997 / McGraw Hill Publishers

Connecting*
Dr. J. Robert Clinton and Paul Stanley / 1992 / NavPress

The Fine Art of Mentoring
Dr. Ted Engstrom / 1989 / Wolgemuth and Hyatt Publishers

As Iron Sharpens Iron*
Dr. Howard Hendricks / 1995 / Fleming Revell

Developing the Leaders Around You
Dr. John C. Maxwell / 1995 / Thomas Nelson Publishers

Mentoring*
Bobb Biehl / 1996 / Broadman and Holman

Let Your Life Speak
Parker Palmer / 2000 / Jossey Bass Publishers

Winning With People
Dr. John C. Maxwell / 2004 / Thomas Nelson Publishers

The Master Plan of Evangelism*
Dr. Robert Coleman / 1963 / Fleming Revell Publishers

Habitudes®: Images That Form Leadership Habits and Attitudes
Dr. Tim Elmore / 2004-2007 / Growing Leaders, Inc.

Nurturing the Leader Within Your Child
Dr. Tim Elmore / 2001, 2008 / Thomas Nelson Publishers

Lifelines: Becoming the Life-Giving Mentor Your Students Need (Training Kit)
Dr. Tim Elmore / 2007 / Growing Leaders, Inc.

* Denotes a book for faith-based communities

mentor match-ups profile

Name _____ Phone _____

Address/City/Zip _____

_____

Age ___ Sex ___ Birthday _____ Marital Status _____

Are you looking for (please circle one):
A Mentor   A Mentee

personal profile

Hobbies/Interests _____

Personality Profile _____

Motivational Needs   _____

Leadership Style ___   _____

Spiritual Gifts _____

How often do you want to meet with a partner in a mentoring relationship? (circle)

Once a week   Twice a week   Once a month   Twice a month

Past discipleship/mentoring experience:

Goals: List three things you'd like to accomplish with the help of mentor/mentee:

1.

2.

3.

FOR MENTORS ONLY
List three areas of strength you can pass on to someone, modeling leadership, finance and budget, decision making, parenting, organization, priority setting, etc.

1.

2.

3.

In their book, *Connecting*, Paul Stanley and Robert Clinton outline seven different kinds of mentoring roles. To help us properly match you with someone, please circle one or two roles for which you feel best suited.

1. DIRECTOR
This mentor provides personal/career direction, accountability, insight for maturation.

2. CONSULTANT
This mentor is on-call as important decisions are made; meeting at forks in the road.

3. COACH
The mentor who offers motivation and skills needed to meet a task or a challenge.

4. TEACHER
The mentor who gives wisdom, understanding and knowledge on a given subject.

5. COUNSELOR
This mentor furnishes big picture perspective; they give a 35,000 foot fly over to life.

6. SPONSOR
The mentor connects a mentee with resources: a personal network, a book, an article.

7. MODEL
The mentor who exemplifies a model life or career; they incarnate the principles in their lifestyle.

FOR MENTEES ONLY
List three areas in which you would most appreciate the help of a mentor, such as time management, parenting, education, spiritual values, career choices, relationships, etc.

1.

2.

3.

CONCERNS AND COMMENTS
Any final communication that will foster a good mentor match up…

personality profile

Directions – In each of the following rows of four words across, place an X in front of the one word that most often applies to you. Continue through all forty lines. Be sure each number is marked.

STRENGTHS

___Adventurous	___Adaptable	___Animated	___Analytical
___Persistent	___Playful	___Persuasive	___Peaceful
___Submissive	___Self-sacrificing	___Sociable	___Strong-willed
___Considerate	___Controlled	___Competitive	___Convincing
___Refreshing	___Respectful	___Reserved	___Resourceful
___Satisfied	___Sensitive	___Self-reliant	___Spirited
___Planner	___Patient	___Positive	___Promoter
___Sure	___Spontaneous	___Scheduled	___Shy
___Orderly	___Obliging	___Outspoken	___Optimistic
___Friendly	___Faithful	___Funny	___Forceful
___Daring	___Delightful	___Diplomatic	___Detailed
___Cheerful	___Consistent	___Cultured	___Confident
___Idealistic	___Independent	___Inoffensive	___Inspiring
___Demonstrative	___Decisive	___Dry humor	___Deep
___Mediator	___Musical	___Mover	___Mixes easily
___Thoughtful	___Tenacious	___Talker	___Tolerant
___Listener	___Loyal	___Leader	___Lively
___Contented	___Chief	___Chartmaker	___Cute
___Perfectionist	___Permissive	___Productive	___Popular
___Bouncy	___Bold	___Behaved	___Balanced

WEAKNESSES

___Blank	___Bashful	___Brassy	___Bossy
___Undisciplined	___Unsympathetic	___Unenthusiastic	___Unforgiving
___Reticent	___Resentful	___Resistant	___Repetitious
___Fussy	___Fearful	___Forgetful	___Frank
___Impatient	___Insecure	___Indecisive	___Interrupts
___Unpopular	___Uninvolved	___Unpredictable	___Unaffectionate
___Headstrong	___Haphazard	___Hard to please	___Hesitant
___Plain	___Pessimistic	___Proud	___Permissive
___Angered easily	___Aimless	___Argumentative	___Alienated
___Naïve	___Negative	___Nervy	___Nonchalant
___Worrier	___Withdrawn	___Workaholic	___Wants credit
___Too sensitive	___Tactless	___Timid	___Talkative
___Doubtful	___Disorganized	___Domineering	___Depressed
___Inconsistent	___Introvert	___Intolerant	___Indifferent
___Messy	___Moody	___Mumbles	___Manipulative
___Slow	___Stubborn	___Show-off	___Skeptical
___Loner	___Lord over	___Lazy	___Loud
___Sluggish	___Suspicious	___Short-tempered	___Scatterbrained
___Revengeful	___Restless	___Reluctant	___Rash
___Compromising	___Critical	___Crafty	___Changeable

Now transfer all your X's to the corresponding words on the personality scoring sheet and add up your totals. Reprinted from PERSONALITY PLUS, Florence Littauer, Flemming H. Revell Publishers.

personality profile scoring sheet

STRENGTHS

Sanguine	Choleric	Melancholy	Phlegmatic
__Adventurous	__Adaptable	__Animated	__Analytical
__Persistent	__Playful	__Persuasive	__Peaceful
__Submissive	__Self-sacrificing	__Sociable	__Strong-willed
__Considerate	__Controlled	__Competitive	__Convincing
__Refreshing	__Respectful	__Reserved	__Resourceful
__Satisfied	__Sensitive	__Self-reliant	__Spirited
__Planner	__Patient	__Positive	__Promoter
__Sure	__Spontaneous	__Scheduled	__Shy
__Orderly	__Obliging	__Outspoken	__Optimistic
__Friendly	__Faithful	__Funny	__Forceful
__Daring	__Delightful	__Diplomatic	__Detailed
__Cheerful	__Consistent	__Cultured	__Confident
__Idealistic	__Independent	__Inoffensive	__Inspiring
__Demonstrative	__Decisive	__Dry humor	__Deep
__Mediator	__Musical	__Mover	__Mixes easily
__Thoughtful	__Tenacious	__Talker	__Tolerant
__Listener	__Loyal	__Leader	__Lively
__Contented	__Chief	__Chartmaker	__Cute
__Perfectionist	__Permissive	__Productive	__Popular
__Bouncy	__Bold	__Behaved	__Balanced
__	__	__	__ TOTALS

WEAKNESSES

__Blank	__Bashful	__Brassy	__Bossy
__Undisciplined	__Unsympathetic	__Unenthusiastic	__Unforgiving
__Reticent	__Resentful	__Resistant	__Repetitious
__Fussy	__Fearful	__Forgetful	__Frank
__Impatient	__Insecure	__Indecisive	__Interrupts
__Unpopular	__Uninvolved	__Unpredictable	__Unaffectionate
__Headstrong	__Haphazard	__Hard to please	__Hesitant
__Plain	__Pessimistic	__Proud	__Permissive
__Angered easily	__Aimless	__Argumentative	__Alienated
__Naïve	__Negative	__Nervy	__Nonchalant
__Worrier	__Withdrawn	__Workaholic	__Wants credit
__Too sensitive	__Tactless	__Timid	__Talkative
__Doubtful	__Disorganized	__Domineering	__Depressed
__Inconsistent	__Introvert	__Intolerant	__Indifferent
__Messy	__Moody	__Mumbles	__Manipulative
__Slow	__Stubborn	__Show-off	__Skeptical
__Loner	__Lord over	__Lazy	__Loud
__Sluggish	__Suspicious	__Short-tempered	__Scatterbrained
__Revengeful	__Restless	__Reluctant	__Rash
__Compromising	__Critical	__Crafty	__Changeable
__	__	__	__ TOTALS
__	__	__	__ COMBINED

189

motivational needs survey

1. Describe a recent job situation in which you experienced a sense of satisfaction and fulfillment.

Identify the closest match of your situation to the choices listed below:
   ° A specific goal was accomplished
   ° Warm, fulfilling relationships were established
   ° A group of people were influenced

2. If you could choose between three work-related projects in which to participate over the next several months, select the one you would enjoy the most:
   ° A project in which you have responsibility for finding the solution to a chronic problem in your organization
   ° A project requiring a cooperative effort with your peer group
   ° A project requiring you to direct and control the efforts of a group of people

3. In your day-to-day job situation, which option provides you the greatest sense of satisfaction?
   ° Taking a calculated risk and seeing it payoff
   ° Being accepted and liked by a group
   ° Giving direction and supervision

4. On a weekly basis, what do you look forward to doing the most?
   ° Finding solutions to problems which prevent goals from being reached
   ° Promoting harmonious working relationships among those in your work group
   ° Using persuasive skills to influence the work of others

5. Your closest associate or friend would describe you as a person who:
   ° Looks for greater challenges
   ° Makes friends and acquaintances easily
   ° Likes to participate in a good argument

6. What would be the most important factor in helping you accomplish your job?
   ° Concrete feedback on how you are doing
   ° An opportunity to interact with others
   ° The amount of authority you can exercise

7. Describe the ingredients you would build into your ideal job assignment. Select the closest match of the most important ingredient with the following choices:
    ° Offers an opportunity to accomplish something significant
    ° Provides an opportunity to work as part of a team
    ° Offers you an opportunity to significantly influence the efforts of others

8. At the end of a project what type of reward would you prefer?
    ° Personal satisfaction in knowing that a goal has been reached
    ° Respect and admiration from your work group
    ° Recognition and advancement through the formal organization

9. When you daydream what do you tend to think about?
    ° Accomplishing new and challenging goals
    ° Warm, friendly relationships within the organization
    ° Rising to the top of the organization

10. In a group situation which would you prefer?
    ° To make the greatest contribution of the group
    ° To be the best liked person in the group
    ° To be the leader of the group

score

	A	B	C
10	—	—	—
9	—	—	—
8	—	—	—
7	—	—	—
6	—	—	—
5	—	—	—
4	—	—	—
3	—	—	—
2	—	—	—
1	—	—	—

MOTIVATIONAL NEEDS DESCRIPTION

Achievement Motivation (A)
1. Tends to spend time thinking of goals and how they can be attained
2. Has an attraction for finding solutions to problems
3. Enjoys taking calculated risks
4. Seeks specific and concrete feedback on the quality of his work
5. Eagerly accepts more responsibility and challenging tasks

Affiliation Motivation (B)
1. Tends to spend time thinking of warm, fulfilling relationships
2. Promotes harmonious situations vs. Conflict within relationships
3. Finds or desires satisfaction from being liked and accepted in the group
4. Seeks situations which require working in cooperation with others
5. Tends to make friends easily

Influence Motivation (C)
1. Tends to spend time thinking of how to influence others or how to control the means of influencing others
2. Seeks positions of leadership in social or work groups
3. Desires to give direction vs. taking orders
4. Tends to be verbally expressive and enjoys a good argument
5. Seeks high status positions or positions requiring persuasive skills

Our Covenant

I commit myself this day to become an effective mentee and life-long learner. I will give myself to reaching my full potential and becoming all that I can become.

In order to reach this goal, I understand that I must be prepared in some specific areas. My character must be polished. My gifts must be developed. My passion must be focused. My attitudes and lifestyle must be groomed.

I agree to participate in a mentoring experience, meeting with my mentor/partner as scheduled on a regular basis. I recognize that my mentor is only a tool in God's hands. I plan, however, to follow through on all lessons and assignments so I can grow into a leader others can trust. I plan to submit to the accountability of my mentor and/or partner. I purpose to finish well, regardless of my human tendency to seek shortcuts or simply quit. I resolve to find my own person to mentor once we've completed this commitment.

I sign this covenant, and purpose to use this experience to make me the person I was meant to be.

Signed: _____ **Date:** _____
                         Mentee

Signed: _____ **Date:** _____
                         Mentor

MENTORING COVENANT GUIDELINES

Your covenant is an agreement to work toward common stated goals. Use this tool to stimulate yourselves to press on toward your goals and vision.

1. Be sure to exchange all necessary information for contact and communication (phone numbers, address, fax numbers, e-mail address, etc.).

2. Define your purpose and goals. List 3-5 goals you plan to accomplish. Be sure to clarify your expectations for this mentoring relationship. Unmet expectations are deadly to the health and growth of a mentoring relationship and ministry.

3. Discuss the Mentor's areas of strengths. Discuss the Mentee's areas of need and expectations.

4. Discuss the seven kinds of mentors and make sure that the mentor's strengths match the mentee's needs.

Use this guide to help determine the kind of mentoring that will take place.

1. Determine when and how often you will meet.

2. Agree together how you will hold each other accountable and responsible. This is a crucial step for the health and success of your mentoring relationship.

3. Confidentiality represents a sacred trust between two parties. Discuss this component with understanding and ultimate agreement.

4. The length and life cycle of a mentoring relationship will vary to some degree. Realize the need to set a reasonable length of time to be involved. Avoid open-ended relationships. Build in periodic times for evaluation. Focus on a one-year commitment.

5. "Begin with the end in mind." Strive to have a healthy closing to the official relationship. Celebrate what God has done and make plans to find another "faithful [person] who will teach [mentor] others also."

a culture that mentors leaders

Let me suggest a process to mentor leaders, on your campus. This is sort of an "accelerated leader development" plan, to use each year with staff and students. It is based on some of the best programs I've seen on campuses across the U.S. In addition to strong support from your top administration, you should include the following basic ingredients:

1. CRITERIA
I suggest you first decide what you believe a leader should look like. What are the core qualities you want to foster in students? Then, create a screen for selecting candidates with leadership potential. While you may invite all students to an event, you should strongly encourage those who are most ready. The best mentors in history chose their mentees.

2. CATALYST
Plan an event that will sufficiently cast a vision for life-on-life mentoring or servant leadership. It may be a single evening or a weekend event. It must be compelling, creative and simple. Be sure to include a vehicle for students to respond at the end, regarding their interests in leadership.

3. COMMUNITIES
At the conclusion of the catalytic event, allow those who wish to be mentored (or grow as a leader) to sign up as they exit. Then, place the interested students in mentoring communities, where they will grow and learn together.

4. CHALLENGE
Come up with a significant problem to be solved or challenge on campus which should be addressed. You might choose a group of challenges/issues that form the context of your process (i.e. people to be moved, problems to be solved). It's optimal if they are real, not hypothetical.

5. COACHES
These are the people who will assist and facilitate the learning. At first, these could be staff, but later you might add students, who've experienced the process. Your coaches are the key to the experience — and will grow in their own leadership skills along the way.

6. CONSULTANTS
Allow students to have exposure to internal and external experts in a variety of subject matter. These are quality leaders on campus or in the community who aren't required to give lots of time but can other wise counsel as needed for the emerging leaders Consultants may come in for just one meeting.

7. CURRICULUM
Provide a tool or resource that enables students to discuss and draw good conclusions about leadership along the way. Often, a bad experience can lead to a bad conclusion and a failure to see a principle at work. This resource should equip and foster interaction.

8. CHAMPION
This person is the orchestrator of the leader development process. If you are to create a leadership culture or a mentoring culture, someone must be the "champion" to wave the flag and cast the vision each year. Eventually, it must be a staff person if the culture is to remain.

hungry for more?

This is just one book offered by Growing Leaders. Check out our other resources, including the Habitudes® series mentioned in this book. We also offer a mentor training Kit called, Lifelines: Becoming the Life-Giving Mentor Your Students Need. Growing Leaders creates these resources for one purpose: to enable you to leverage your influence effectively and transform our society.

Growing Leaders is committed to equipping the next generation of leaders, who will change the world. We want to transform people from the inside out, so they can turn their world upside down. This book is one of many resources, which equips you to lead and mentor in a healthy, effective way. We have a variety of tools to help you learn to lead, while you experience community. Some of those tools are:

* Student Leadership Training Forum
* A National Leadership Forum
* Videos, CDs and workbooks
* Events held on your campus
* Free electronic subscriptions

Our goal is to partner with you to help nurture a leadership culture on your campus or in your organization. Visit our website for ideas on how to begin that process for faculty, staff and students.

www.GrowingLeaders.com